The Guide to Reading

by Dr. Lyman Abbott and Asa Don Dickenson

THE POCKET UNIVERSITY

THE GUIDE TO READING

EDITED BY DR. LYMAN ABBOTT, ASA DON DICKINSON AND OTHERS

CONTENTS

THE POCKET UNIVERSITY Books for Study and Reading BY LYMAN ABBOTT

There are three services which books may render in the home: they may be ornaments, tools, or friends.

I was told a few years ago the following story which is worth retelling as an illustration of the use of books as ornaments. A millionaire who had one house in the city, one in the mountains, and one in the South, wished to build a fourth house on the seashore. A house ought to have a library. Therefore this new house was to have a library. When the house was finished he found the library shelves had been made so shallow that they would not take books of an ordinary size. His architect proposed to change the bookshelves. The millionaire did not wish the change made, but told his architect to buy fine bindings of classical books and glue them into the shelves. The architect on making inquiries discovered that the bindings would cost more than slightly shop-worn editions of the books themselves. So the books were bought, cut in two from top to bottom about in the middle, one half thrown away, and the other half replaced upon the shelves that the handsome backs presented the same appearance they would have presented if the entire book had been there. Then the glass doors were locked, the key to the glass doors lost, and sofas and chairs and tables put against them. Thus the millionaire has his library furnished with handsome bindings and these I may add are quite adequate for all the use which he wishes to make of them.

This is a rather extreme case of the use of books as ornaments, but it illustrates in a bizarre way what is a not uncommon use. There is this to be said for that illiterate millionaire: well-bound books are excellent ornaments. No decoration with wall paper or fresco can make a parlor as attractive as it can be made with low bookshelves filled with works of standard authors and leaving room above for statuary, or pictures, or the inexpensive decoration of flowers picked from one's own garden. I am inclined to think that the most attractive parlor I have ever visited is that of a bookish friend whose walls are thus furnished with what not only delights the eye, but silently invites the mind to an inspiring companionship.

More important practically than their use as ornaments is the use of books as tools. Every professional man needs his special tools--the lawyer his law books, the doctor his medical books, the minister his theological treatises and his Biblical helps. I can always tell when I go into a clergyman's study by looking at his books whether he is living in the Twentieth Century or in the Eighteenth. Tools do not make the man, but they make his work and so show what the man is.

Every home ought to have some books that are tools and the children should be taught how to use them. There should be at least an atlas, a dictionary, and an encyclopedia. If in the evening when the family talk about the war in the Balkans the father gets out the atlas and the children look to see where Roumania and Bulgaria and Greece and Constantinople and the

Dardanelles are on the map, they will learn more of real geography in half an hour than they will learn in a week of school study concerning countries in which they have no interest. When there is reading aloud in the family circle, if every unfamiliar word is looked up in a dictionary, which should always lie easily accessible upon the table, they will get unconsciously a widening of their vocabulary and a knowledge of the use of English which will be an invaluable supplement to the work of their teacher of English in the school. As to cyclopedias they are of all sizes from the little six- volumed cyclopedia in the Everyman's Library to the twenty-nine volumed Encyclopedia Britannica, and from the general cyclopedia with more or less full information on every conceivable topic to the more distinctive family cyclopedia which covers the life of the household. Where there are children in the family the cyclopedia which covers the field they are most apt to be interested in--such as "The Library of Work & Play" or "The Guide Series" to biography, music, pictures, etc. --is the best one to begin with. After they have learned to go to it for information which they want, they will desire a more general cyclopedia because their wants have increased and broadened.

So much for books as ornaments and as tools. Certainly not less important, if comparisons can be made I am inclined to say more important, is their usefulness as friends.

In Smith College this distinction is marked by the College authorities in an interesting and valuable manner. In the library building there is a room for study. It is furnished with a number of plain oak or walnut tables and with chairs which do not invite to repose. There are librarians present to get from the stacks the special books which the student needs. The room is barren of ornament. Each student is hard at --work examining, comparing, collating. She is to be called on to-morrow in class to tell what she has learned, or next week to hand in a thesis the product of her study. All eyes are intent upon the allotted task; no one looks up to see you when you enter. In the same building is another room which I will call The Lounge, though I think it bears a different name. The books are upon shelves around the wall and all are within easy reach. Many of them are fine editions. A wood fire is burning in the great fireplace. The room is furnished with sofas and easy chairs. No one is at work. No one is talking. No! but they are listening--listening to authors whose voices have long since been silent in death.

In every home there ought to be books that are friends. In every day, at least in every week, there ought to be some time which can be spent in cultivating their friendship. This is reading, and reading is very different from study.

The student has been at work all the morning with his tools. He has been studying a question of Constitutional Law: What are the powers of the President of the United States? He has examined the Constitution; then Willoughby or Watson on the Constitution; then he turns to The Federalist; then perhaps to the Constitutional debates, or to the histories, such as Von Holst's Constitutional History of the United States, or to treatises, such as Bryce's American Commonwealth. He compares the different opinions, weighs them, deliberates, endeavors to reach a decision. Wearied with his morning pursuit of truth through a maze of conflicting theories, he puts his tools by and goes to dinner. In the evening he sits down in the same library for an hour with his friends. He selects his friend according to his mood. Macaulay carries him back across the centuries and he lives for an hour with The Puritans or with Dr. Samuel Johnson. Carlyle carries him unharmed for an hour through the exciting scenes of the French Revolution; or he chuckles over the caustic humor of Thackeray's semi-caricatures of English snobs. With Jonathan Swift as a guide he travels with Gulliver into no-man's land and visits Lilliput or Brobdingnag; or Oliver Goldsmith enables him to forget the strenuous life of America by taking him to "The Deserted Village." He joins Charles Lamb's friends, listens to the prose-poet's reveries on Dream-Children, then closes his eyes and falls into a reverie of his own childhood days; or he spends an hour with Tennyson, charmed by his always musical but not often virile verse, or with Browning, inspired by his always virile but often rugged verse, or with Milton or Dante, and forgets this world altogether, with its problems and perplexities, convoyed to another realm by these spiritual guides; or he turns to the autobiography of one of the great men of the past, telling of his achievements, revealing his doubts and difficulties, his self-conflicts and self-victories, and so inspiring the reader to make his own life sublime. Or one of the great scientists may interpret to him the wonders of nature and thrill him with the achievements of man in solving some of the riddles of the universe and winning successive mastery over its splendid forces.

It is true that no dead thing is equal to a living person. The one afternoon I spent in John G. Whittier's home, the one dinner I took with Professor Tyndall in his London home, the one half hour which Herbert Spencer gave to me at his Club, mean more to me than any equal time spent in reading the writings of either one of them. These occasions of personal fellowship abide in the memory as long as life lasts. This I say with emphasis that what I say next may not be misunderstood--that there is one respect in which the book is the best of possible friends. You do not need to decide beforehand what friend you will invite to spend the evening with you. When supper is over and you sit down by the evening lamp for your hour of companionship, you give your invitation according to your inclination at the time. And if you have made a mistake, and the friend you have invited is not the one you want to talk to, you can "shut him up" and not hurt his feelings. Remarkable is the friend who speaks only when you want to listen and can keep silence when you want silence. Who is there who has not been sometimes bored by a good friend who went on talking when you wanted to reflect on what he had already said? Who is there who has not had his patience well nigh exhausted at times by a friend whose enthusiasm for his theme appeared to be quite inexhaustible? A book never bores you because you can always lay it down before it becomes a bore.

Most families can do with a few books that are tools. In these days in which there is a library in almost every village, the family that has an atlas, a dictionary, and a cyclopedia can look to the public library for such other tools as are necessary. And we can depend on the library or the book club for books that are mere acquaintances--the current book about current events, the books that are read to-day and forgotten to-morrow, leaving only a residuum in our memory, the book that, once read, we never expect to read again. In my own home this current literature is either borrowed and returned or, if purchased, as soon as it has been used is passed along to neighbors or to the village library. Its room is better than its company on my over-crowded book shelves.

But books that are friends ought to abide in the home. The very form of the book grows familiar; a different edition, even a different copy, does not quite serve the same friendly purpose. If the reader is wise he talks to his friend as well as listens to him and adds in pencil notes, in the margin or on the back pages of the book, his own reflections. I take up these books marked with the indications of my conversation with my friend and in these pencilled memoranda find an added value. Sometimes the mark emphasizes an agreement between my friend and me, sometimes it emphasizes a disagreement, and sometimes it indicates the progress in thought I have made since last we met. A wisely marked book is sometimes doubled in value by the marking.

Before I bring this essay to a close, already lengthened beyond my predetermined limits, I venture to add four rules which may be of value at least to the casual reader.

For reading, select the book which suits your inclination. In study it is wise to make your will command your mind and go on with your task however unattractive it may prove to you. You may be a Hamiltonian, and Jefferson's views of the Constitution may repel you, or even bore you. No matter. Go on. Scholarship requires persistence in study of matter that repels or even bores the student. You may be a devout believer and Herbert Spencer repellent. Nevertheless, if you are studying you may need to master Herbert Spencer. But if you are reading, read what interests you. If Scott does not interest you and Dickens does, drop Scott and read Dickens. You need not be any one's enemy; but you need not be a friend with everybody. This is as true of books as of persons. For friendship some agreement in temperament is quite essential.

Henry Ward Beecher's application of this principle struck me as interesting and unique. He did a great deal of his reading on the train in his lecture tours. His invariable companion was a black bag and the black bag always contained some books. As I am writing from recollection of a conversation with him some sixty years ago my statement may lack in accuracy of detail, but not, I think, in essential veracity. He selected in the beginning of the year some four departments of reading, such as Poetry, History, Philosophy, Fiction, and in each department a specific course, such as Greek Poetry, Macaulay's History, Spencer's Philosophy, Scott's Novels. Then he read according to his mood, but generally in the selected course: if poetry, the Greek poets; if history, Macaulay; if philosophy, Spencer; if fiction, Scott. This gave at once liberty to his mood and unity to his reading.

One may read either for acquisition or for inspiration. A gentleman who has acquired a national reputation as a popular lecturer and preacher, formed the habit, when in college, of always subjecting himself to a recitation in all his serious reading. After finishing a chapter he would close the book and see how much of what he had read he could recall. One consequence is the development of a quite marvelous memory, the results of which are seen in frequent and felicitous references in his public speaking to literature both ancient and modern.

He who reads for inspiration pursues a different course. If as he reads, a thought expressed by his author starts a train of thought in his own mind, he lays down his book and follows his thought wherever it may lead him. He endeavors to remember, not the thought which the author has recorded, but the unrecorded thought which the author has stimulated in his own mind. Reading is to him not an acquisition but a ferment. I imagine from my acquaintance with Phillips Brooks and with his writings that this was his method.

I have a friend who says that he prefers to select his authors for himself, not to have them selected for him. But he has money with which to buy the books he wants, a room in which to put them, and the broad culture which enables him to make a wise selection. Most of us lack one at least of these qualifications: the money, the space, or the knowledge. For most of us a library for the home, selected as this Pocket Library has been has three great advantages: the cost is not prohibitive; the space can easily be made in out home for the books; and the selection is more wisely made than any we could make for ourselves. For myself I should be very glad to have the editors of this series come into my library, which is fairly large but sadly needs weeding out, give me a literary appraisal of my books, and tell me what volumes in their respective departments they think I could best dispense with to make room for their betters, and what their betters would be.

To these considerations in favor of such a home library as this, may be added the fact that the books are of such a size that one can easily put a volume in his pocket when he is going on a train or in a trolley car. For busy men and women often the only time for reading is the time which too many of us are apt to waste in doing nothing.

Perhaps the highest use of good books is their use as friends. Such a wisely selected group of friends as this library furnishes is an invaluable addition to any home which receives it and knows how to make wise use of it. I am glad to have the privilege of introducing it and hope that this introduction may add to the number of homes in which it will find a welcome.

THE PURPOSE OF READING

BY JOHN MACY

Why do we read books is one of those vast questions that need no answer. As well ask, Why ought we to be good? or, Why do we believe in a God? The whole universe of wisdom answers. To attempt an answer in a single article would be like turning a spyglass for a moment toward the stars. We take the great simple things for granted, like the air we breathe. In a country that holds popular education to be the foundation of all its liberties and fortunes, we do not find many people who need to be argued into the belief that the reading of books is good for us; even people who do not read much acknowledge vaguely that they ought to read more.

There are, to be sure, men of rough worldly wisdom, even endowed with spiritual insight, who distrust "book learning" and fall back on the obvious truth that experience of life is the great teacher. Such persons are in a measure justified in their conviction by the number of unwise human beings who have read much but to no purpose.

The bookful blockhead, ignorantly read, With loads of learned lumber in his head is a living argument against mere reading. But we can meet such argument by pointing out that the blockhead who cannot learn from books cannot learn much from life, either. That sometimes useful citizen whom it is fashionable to call a Philistine, and who calls himself a "practical man," often has under him a beginner fresh from the schools, who is glib and confident in repeating bookish theories, but is not yet skillful in applying them. If the practical man is thoughtless, he sniffs at theory and points to his clumsy assistant as proof of the uselessness of what is to be got from books. If he is wise, the practical man realizes how much better off he would be, how much farther his hard work and experience might have carried him, if he had had the advantage of bookish training.

Moreover, the hard-headed skeptic, self-made and self-secure, who will not traffic with the literature that touches his life work, is seldom so confined to his own little shop that he will not, for recreation, take holiday tours into the literature of other men's lives and labors. The man who does not like to read any books is, I am confident, seldom found, and at the risk of slandering a patriot, I will express the doubt whether he is a good citizen. Honest he may be, but certainly not wise. The human race for thousands of years has been writing its experiences, telling how it has met our everlasting problems, how it has struggled with darkness and rejoiced in light. What fools we should be to try to live our lives without the guidance and inspiration of the generations that have gone before, without the joy, encouragement, and sympathy that the best imaginations of our generation are distilling into words. For literature is simply life selected and condensed into books. In a few hours we can follow all that is recorded of the life of Jesus--the best that He did in years of teaching and suffering all ours for a day of reading, and the more deeply ours for a lifetime of reading and meditation!

If the expression of life in words is strong and beautiful and true it outlives empires, like the oldest books of the Old Testament. If it is weak or trivial or untrue, it is forgotten like most of the "stories" in yesterday's newspaper, like most of the novels of last year. The expression of truth, the transmission of knowledge and emotions between man and man from generation to generation, these are the purposes of literature. Not to read books is like being shut up in a dungeon while life rushes by outside.

I happen to be writing in Christmas week, and I have read for the tenth time "A Christmas Carol," by Dickens, that amazing allegory in which the hard, bitter facts of life are involved in a beautiful myth, that wizard's caldron in which humor bubbles and from which rise phantom figures of religion and poetry. Can any one doubt that if this story were read by every man, woman, and child in the world, Christmas would be a happier time and the feelings of the race elevated and strengthened? The story has power enough to defeat armies, to make revolutions in the faith of men, and turn the cold markets of the world into festival scenes of charity. If you know any mean person you may be sure that he has not read "A Christmas Carol," or that he read it long ago and has forgotten it. I know there are persons who pretend that the sentimentality of Dickens destroys their interest in him. I once took a course with an over-refined, imperfectly educated professor of literature, who advised me that in time I should outgrow my liking for Dickens. It was only his way of recommending to me a kind of fiction that I had not learned to like. In time I did learn to like it, but I did not outgrow Dickens. A person who can read "A Christmas Carol" aloud to the end and keep his voice steady is, I suspect, not a safe person to trust with one's purse or one's honor.

It is not necessary to argue about the value of literature or even to define it.

One way of bringing ourselves to realize vividly what literature can do for us is to enter the libraries of great men and see what books have done for the acknowledged leaders of our race.

You will recall John Stuart Mill's experience in reading Wordsworth. Mill was a man of letters as well as a scientific economist and philosopher, and we expect to find that men of letters have been nourished on literature; reading must necessarily have been a large part of their professional preparation. The examples of men of action who have been molded and inspired by books will perhaps be more helpful to remember; for most of us are not to be writers or to engage in purely intellectual work; our ambitions point to a thousand different careers in the world of action.

Lincoln was not primarily a man of letters, although he wrote noble prose on occasion, and the art of expression was important, perhaps indispensable, in his political success. He read deeply in the law and in books on public questions. For general literature he had little time, either during his early struggles or after his public life began, and his autobiographical memorandum contains the significant words: "Education defective." But these more significant words are found in a letter which he wrote to Hackett, the player: "Some of Shakespeare's plays I have never read, while others I have gone over perhaps as frequently as any unprofessional reader. Among the latter are 'Lear,' 'Richard III,' 'Henry VIII,' 'Hamlet,' and, especially, 'Macbeth.'"

If he had not read these masterpieces, no doubt he would have become President just the same and guided the country through its terrible difficulties; but we may be fairly sure that the high philosophy by which he lifted the political differences of his day above partisan quarrels, the command of words which gives his letters and speeches literary permanence apart from their biographical interest, the poetic exaltation of the Gettysburg Address, these higher qualities of genius, beyond the endowment of any native wit, came to Lincoln in some part from the reading of books. It is important to note that he followed Franklin's advice to read much but not too many books;

the list of books mentioned in the biographical records of Lincoln is not long. But he went over those half dozen plays "frequently." We should remember, too, that he based his ideals upon the Bible and his style upon the King James Version. His writings abound in Biblical phrases.

We are accustomed to regard Lincoln as a thinker. His right arm in the saddest duty of his life, General Grant, was a man of deeds; as Lincoln said of him, he was a "copious worker and fighter, but a very meager writer and telegrapher." In his "Memoirs," Grant makes a modest confession about his reading:

"There is a fine library connected with the Academy [West Point] from which cadets can get books to read in their quarters. I devoted more time to these than to books relating to the course of studies. Much of the time, I am sorry to say, was devoted to novels, but not those of a trashy sort. I read all of Bulwer's then published, Cooper's, Marryat's, Scott's, Washington Irving's works, Lever's, and many others that I do not now remember."

Grant was not a shining light in his school days, nor indeed in his life until the Civil War, and at first sight he is not a striking example of a great man influenced by books. Yet who can deny that the fruit of that early reading is to be found in his "Memoirs," in which a man of action, unused to writing, and called upon to narrate great events, discovers an easy adequate style? There is a dangerous kind of conjecture in which many biographers indulge when they try to relate logically the scattered events of a man's life. A conjectured relation is set down as a proved or unquestioned relation. I have said something about this in [Footnote: See John Macy's Guide to Reading, Chapter VIII.] writing on biography, and I do not wish to violate my own teachings. But we may, without harm, hazard the suggestion, which is only a suggestion, that some of the chivalry of Scott's heroes wove itself into Grant's instincts and inspired this businesslike, modern general, in the days when politeness has lost some of its flourish, to be the great gentleman he was at Appomattox when he quietly wrote into the terms of the surrender that the Confederate officers should keep their side arms. Stevenson's account of the episode in his essay on "Gentlemen" is heightened, though not above the dignity of the facts, certainly not to a degree that is untrue to the facts, as they are to be read in Grant's simple narrative. Since I have agreed not to say "ought to read," I will only express the hope that the quotation from Stevenson will lead you to the essay and to the volume that contains it.

"On the day of the capitulation, Lee wore his presentation sword; it was the first thing that Grant observed, and from that moment he had but one thought: how to avoid taking it. A man, who should perhaps have had the nature of an angel, but assuredly not the special virtues of a gentleman, might have received the sword, and no more words about it; he would have done well in a plain way. One who wished to be a gentleman, and knew not how, might have received and returned it: he would have done infamously ill, he would have proved himself a cad; taking the stage for himself, leaving to his adversary confusion of countenance and the ungraceful posture of a man condemned to offer thanks. Grant without a word said, added to the terms this article: 'All officers to retain their side arms'; and the problem was solved and Lee kept his sword, and Grant went down to posterity, not perhaps a fine gentleman, but a great one."

Napoleon, who of all men of mighty deeds after Julius Caesar had the greatest intellect, was a tireless reader, and since he needed only four or five hours' sleep in twenty-four he found time to read in the midst of his prodigious activities. Nowadays those of us who are preparing to conquer the world are taught to strengthen ourselves for the task by getting plenty of sleep. Napoleon's devouring eyes read far into the night; when he was in the field his secretaries forwarded a stream of books to his headquarters; and if he was left without a new volume to begin, some underling had to bear his imperial displeasure. No wonder that his brain contained so many ideas that, as the sharp- tongued poet, Heine, said, one of his lesser thoughts would keep all the scholars and professors in Germany busy all their lives making commentaries on it.

In Franklin's "Autobiography" we have an unusually clear statement of the debt of a man of affairs to literature: "From a child I was fond of reading, and all the little money that came into my hands was ever laid out in books. Pleased with the 'Pilgrim's Progress,' my first collection was of John Bunyan's works in separate little volumes.... My father's little library consisted chiefly of books on polemic divinity, most of which I read, and have since often regretted that, at a time when I had such a thirst for knowledge, more proper books had not fallen in my way, since it was now resolved that I should not be a clergyman. 'Plutarch's Lives' there was in which I read abundantly, and I still think that time spent to great advantage. There was also a book of De Foe's, called an 'Essay on Projects,' and another of Dr. Mather's, called 'Essays to do Good,' which perhaps gave me a turn of thinking that had an influence on some of the principal future events of my life."

It is not surprising to find that the most versatile of versatile Americans read De Foe's "Essay on Projects," which contains practical suggestions on a score of subjects, from banking and insurance to national academics. In Cotton Mather's "Essays to do Good" is the germ perhaps of the sensible morality of Franklin's "Poor Richard." The story of how Franklin pave his nights to the study of Addison and by imitating the Spectator papers taught himself to write, is the best of lessons in self-cultivation in English. The "Autobiography" is proof of how well he learned, not Addison's style, which was suited to Joseph Addison and not to Benjamin Franklin, but a clear, firm manner of writing. In Franklin's case we can see not only what he owed to books, but how one side of his fine, responsive mind was starved because, as he put it, more proper books did not fall in his way. The blind side of Franklin's great intellect was his lack of religious imagination. This defect may be accounted for by the forbidding nature of the religious books in his father's library. Repelled by the dull discourses, the young man missed the religious exaltation and poetic mysticism which the New England divines concealed in their polemic argument. Franklin's liking for Bunyan and his confession that his father's discouragement kept him from being a poet--"most probably," he says, "a very bad one"--show that he would have responded to the right kind of religious literature, and not have remained all his life such a complacent rationalist.

If it is clear that the purpose of reading is to put ourselves in communication with the best minds of our race, we need go no farther for a definition of "good reading." Whatever human beings hare said well is literature, whether it be the Declaration of Independence or a love story. Reading consists in nothing more than in taking one of the volumes in which somebody has said something well, opening it on one's knee, and beginning.

We take it for granted, then, that we know why we read. We may ask one further question: How shall we read? One answer is that we should read with as much of ourselves as a book warrants, with the part of ourselves that a book demands. Mrs. Browning says:

We get no good By being ungenerous, even to a book, And calculating profits--so much help By so much reading. It is rather when We gloriously forget ourselves, and plunge Soul-forward, headlong, into a book's profound, Impassioned for its beauty, and salt of truth-- 'Tis then we get the right good from a book.

We sometimes know exactly what we wish to get from a book, especially if it is a volume of information on a definite subject. But the great book is full of treasures that one does not deliberately seek, and which indeed one may miss altogether on the first journey through. It is almost nonsensical to say: Read Macaulay for clearness, Carlyle for power, Thackeray for ease. Literary excellence is not separated and bottled up in any such drug-shop array. If Macaulay is a master of clearness it is because he is much else besides. Unless we read a man for all there is in him, we get very little; we meet, not a living human being, not a vital book, but something dead, dismembered, disorganized. We do not read Thackeray for ease; we read him for Thackeray and enjoy his ease by the way.

We must read a book for all there is in it or we shall get little or nothing. To be masters of books we must have learned to let books master us. This is true of books that we are required to read, such as text-books, and of those we read voluntarily and at leisure. The law of reading is to give a book its due and a little more. The art of reading is to know how to apply this law. For there is an art of reading, for each of us to learn for himself, a private way of making the acquaintance of books.

Macaulay, whose mind was never hurried or confused, learned to read very rapidly, to absorb a page at a glance. A distinguished professor, who has spent his life in the most minutely technical scholarship, surprised us one day by commending to his classes the fine art of "skipping." Many good books, including some most meritorious "three- decker" novels, have their profitless pages, and it is useful to know by a kind of practised instinct where to pause and reread and where to run lightly and rapidly over the page. It is a useful accomplishment not only in the reading of fiction, but in the business of life, to the man of affairs who must get the gist of a mass of written matter, and to the student of any special subject.

Usually, of course, a book that is worth reading at all is worth reading carefully. Thoroughness of reading is the first thing to preach and to practise, and it is perhaps dangerous to suggest to a beginner that any book should be skimmed. The suggestion will serve its purpose if it indicates that there are ways to read, that practice in reading is like practice in anything else; the more one does, and the more intelligently one does it, the farther and more easily one can go. In the best reading--that is, the most thoughtful reading of the most thoughtful books--attention is necessary. It is even necessary that we should read some works, some passages, so often and with such close application that we commit them to memory. It is said that the habit of learning pieces by heart is not so prevalent as it used to be. I hope that this is not so. What! have you no poems by heart, no great songs, no verses from the Bible, no speeches from Shakespeare? Then you have not begun to read, you have not learned how to read.

We have said enough, perhaps, of the theories of reading. The one lesson that seems most obvious is that we must come close to literature.

HOW TO GET THE BEST OUT OF BOOKS

By RICHARD LE GALLIENNE

One is sometimes asked by young people panting after the waterbrooks of knowledge: "How shall I get the best out of books?" Here indeed, is one of those questions which can be answered only in general terms, with possible illustrations from one's own personal experience. Misgivings, too, as to one's fitness to answer it may well arise, as wistfully looking round one's own bookshelves, one asks oneself: "Have I myself got the best out of this wonderful world of books?" It is almost like asking oneself: "Have I got the best out of life?"

As we make the survey, it will surely happen that our eyes fall on many writers whom the stress of life, or spiritual indolence, has prevented us from using as all the while they have been eager to be used; friends we might have made yet never have made, neglected counsellors we would so often have done well to consult, guides that could have saved us many a wrong turning in the difficult way. There, in unvisited corners of our shelves, what neglected fountains of refreshments, gardens in which we have never walked, hills we have never climbed!

"Well," we say with a sigh, "a man cannot read everything; it is life that has interrupted our studies, and probably the fact is that we have accumulated more books than we really need." The young reader's appetite is largely in his eyes, and it is very natural for one who is born with a taste for books to gather them about him at first indiscriminately, on the hearsay recommendation of fame, before he really knows what his own individual tastes are, or are going to be, and in that wistful survey I have imagined, our eyes will fall, too, with some amusement, on not a few volumes to which we never have had any really personal relation, and which, whatever their distinction or their value for others, were never meant for us. The way to do with such books is to hand them over to some one who has a use for them. On our shelves they are like so much good thrown away, invitations to entertainments for which we have no taste. In all vital libraries, such a process of progressive refection is continually going on, and to realize what we do not want in books, or cannot use, must, obviously, be a first principle in our getting the best out of them.

Yes, we read too many books, and too many that, as they do not really interest us, bring us neither benefit nor diversion. Even from the point of view of reading for pleasure, we manage our reading badly. We listlessly allow ourselves to be bullied by publishers' advertisements into reading the latest fatuity in fiction, without, in one case out of twenty, finding any of that pleasure we are ostensibly seeking. Instead, indeed, we are bored and enervated, where we might have been refreshed, either by romance or laughter. Such reading resembles the idle absorption of innocuous but interesting beverages, which cheer as little as they inebriate, and yet at the same time make frivolous demands on the digestive functions. No one but a publisher could call such reading "light." Actually it is weariness to the flesh and heaviness to the spirit.

If, therefore, our idea of the best in books is the recreation they can so well bring; if we go to books as to a playground to forget our cares and to blow off the cobwebs of business, let us make sure that we find what we seek. It is there, sure enough. The playgrounds of literature are indeed wide, and alive with bracing excitement, nor is there any limit to the variety of the games. But let us be sure, when we set Out to be amused, that we really are amused, that our humorists do really make us laugh, and that our story-tellers have stories to tell and know how to tell them. Beware of imitations, and, when in doubt, try Shakespeare, and Dumas--even Ouida. As a rule, avoid the "spring lists," or "summer reading." "Summer reading" is usually very hot work.

Hackneyed as it is, there is no better general advice on reading than Shakespeare's--

No profit is where is no pleasure taken,

In brief, sir, study what you most affect.

Not only in regard to books whose purpose, frankly, is recreation, but also in regard to the graver uses of books, this counsel no less holds. No reading does us any good that is not a pleasure to us. Her paths are paths of pleasantness. Yet, of course, this does not mean that all profitable reading is easy reading. Some of the books that give us the finest pleasure need the closest application for their enjoyment. There is always a certain spiritual and mental effort necessary to be made before we tackle the great books. One might compare it to the effort of getting up to see the sun rise. It is no little tug to leave one's warm bed--but once we are out in the crystalline morning air, wasn't it worth it? Perhaps our finest pleasure always demands some such austerity of preparation. That is the secret of the truest epicureanism. Books like Dante's "Divine Comedy," or Plato's dialogues, will not give themselves to a lounging reader. They demand a braced, attentive spirit. But when the first effort has been made, how exhilarating are the altitudes in which we find ourselves; what a glow of pure joy is the reward which we are almost sure to win by our mental mountaineering.

But such books are not for moments when we are unwilling or unable to make that necessary effort. We cannot always be in the mood for the great books, and often we are too tired physically, or too low down on the depressed levels of daily life, even to lift our eyes toward the hills. To attempt the great books--or any books at all--in such moods and moments, is a mistake. We may thus contract a prejudice against some writer who, approached in more fortunate moments, would prove the very man we were looking for.

To know when to read is hardly less important than to know what to read. Of course, every one must decide the matter for himself; but one general counsel may be ventured: Read only what you want to read, and only when you want to read it.

Some readers find the early morning, when they have all the world to themselves, their best time for reading, and, if you are a good sleeper, and do not find early rising more wearying than refreshing, there is certainly no other time of the day when the mind is so eagerly receptive, has so keen an edge of appetite, and absorbs a book in so fine an intoxication. For your true book-lover there is no other exhilaration so exquisite as that with which one reads an inspiring book in the solemn freshness of early morning. One's nerves seem peculiarly strung for exquisite impressions in the first dewy hours of the day, there is a virginal sensitiveness and purity about all our senses, and the mere delight of the eye in the printed page is keener than at any other time. "The Muses love the morning, and that is a fit time for study," said Erasmus to his friend Christianus of Lubeck; and, certainly, if early rising agrees with one, there is no better time for getting the very best out of a book. Moreover, morning reading has a way of casting a spell of peace over the whole day. It has a sweet, solemnizing effect on our thoughts--a sort of mental matins--and through the day's business it accompanies us as with hidden music.

There are others who prefer to do their reading at night, and I presume that most readers of this paper are so circumstanced as to have no time to spare for reading during the day. Personally, I think that one of the best places to read in is bed. Paradoxical as it may sound, one is not so apt to fall asleep over his book in bed as in the post-prandial armchair. While one's body rests itself, one's mind, remains alert, and, when the time for sleep comes at last, it passes into unconsciousness, tranquilized and sweetened with thought and pleasantly weary with healthy exercise. One awakens, too, next morning, with, so to say, a very pleasant taste of meditation in the mouth. Erasmus, again, has a counsel for the bedtime reader, expressed with much felicity. "A little before you sleep," he says, "read something that is exquisite, and worth remembering; and contemplate upon it till you fall asleep; and, when you awake in the morning, call yourself to an account for it."

In an old Atlantic Monthly, from which, if I remember aright, he never rescued it, Oliver Wendell Holmes has a delightful paper on the delights of reading in bed, entitled "Pillow-Smoothing Authors."

Then, though I suppose we shall have the oculists against us, the cars are good places to read in--if you have the power of detachment, and are able to switch off your ears from other people's conversation. It is a good plan to have a book with you in all places and at all times. Most likely you will carry it many a day and never give it a single look, but, even so, a book in the hand is always a companionable reminder of that happier world of fancy, which, alas! most of us can only visit by playing truant from the real world. As some men wear boutonnieres, so a reader carries a book, and sometimes, when he is feeling the need of beauty, or the solace of a friend, he opens it, and finds both. Probably he will count among the most fruitful moments of his reading the snatched glimpses of beauty and wisdom he has caught in the morning car. The covers of his book have often proved like some secret door, through which, surreptitiously opened, he has looked for a moment into his own particular fairy land. Never mind the oculist, therefore, but, whenever you feel like it, read in the car.

One or two technical considerations may be dealt with in this place. How to remember what one reads is one of them. Some people are blest with such good memories that they never forget anything that they have once read. Literary history has recorded many miraculous memories. Still, it is quite possible to remember too much, and thus turn one's mind into a lumber-room of useless information. A good reader forgets even more than he remembers. Probably we remember all that is really necessary for us, and, except in so far as our reading is technical and directed toward some exact science or, profession, accuracy of memory is not important. As the Sabbath was made for man, so books were made for the reader, and, when a reader has assimilated from any given book his own proper nourishment and pleasure, the rest of the book is so much oyster shell. The end of true reading is the development of individuality. Like a certain water insect, the reader instinctively selects from the outspread world of books the building materials for the house of his soul. He chooses here and rejects there, and remembers or forgets according to the formative desire of his nature. Yet it often happens that he forgets much that he needs to remember, and thus the question of methodical aids to memory arises.

One's first thought, of course, is of the commonplace book. Well, have you ever kept one, or, to be more accurate, tried to keep one? Personally, I believe in the commonplace book so long as we don't expect too much from it. Its two dangers are (1) that one is apt to make far too many and too minute entries, and (2) that one is apt to leave all the remembering to the commonplace book, with a consequent relaxation of one's own attention. On the other hand, the mere discipline of a commonplace book is a good thing, and if--as I think is the best way--we copy out the passages at full length, they are thus the more securely fixed in the memory. A commonplace book kept with moderation is really useful, and may be delightful. But the entries should be made at full length. Otherwise, the thing becomes a mere index, an index which encourages us to forget.

Another familiar way of assisting one's memory in reading is to mark one's own striking passages. This method is chiefly worth while for the sake of one's second and subsequent readings; though it all depends when one makes the markings--at what time of his life, I mean. Markings made at the age of twenty years are of little use at thirty--except negatively. In fact, I have usually found that all I care to read again of a book read at twenty is just the passages I did not mark. This consideration, however, does not depreciate the value of one's comparatively contemporary markings. At the same time, marking, like indexing, is apt, unless guarded against, to relax the memory. One is apt to mark a passage in lieu of remembering it. Still, for a second reading, as I say--a second reading not too long after the first-- marking is a useful method, particularly if one regards his first reading of a book as a prospecting of the ground rather than a taking possession. One's first reading is a sort of flying visit, during which he notes the places he would like to visit again and really come to know. A brief index of one's markings at the end of a volume is a method of memory that commended itself to the booklovers of former days--to Leigh Hunt, for instance.

Yet none of these external methods, useful as they may prove, can compare with a habit of thorough attention. We read far too hurriedly, too much in the spirit of the "quick lunch." No doubt we do so a great deal from the misleading idea that there is so very much to read. Actually, there is very little to read,--if we wish for real reading-- and there is time to read it all twice over. We--Americans--bolt our books as we do our food, and so get far too little good out of them. We treat our mental digestions as brutally as we treat our stomachs. Meditation is the digestion of the mind, but we allow ourselves no time for meditation. We gorge our eyes with the printed page, but all too little of what we take in with our eyes ever reaches our minds or our spirits. We assimilate what we can from all this hurry of superfluous food, and the rest goes to waste, and, as a natural consequence, contributes only to the wear and tear of our mental organism.

Books should be real things. They were so once, when a man would give a fat field in exchange for a small manuscript; and they are no less real to-day-- some of them. Each age contributes one or two real books to the eternal library--and always the old books remain, magic springs of healing and refreshment. If no one should write a book for a thousand years, there are quite enough books to keep us going. Real books there are in plenty. Perhaps there are more real books than there are real readers. Books are the strong tincture of experience. They are to be taken carefully, drop by drop, not carelessly gulped down by the bottleful. Therefore, if you would get the best out of books, spend a quarter of an hour in reading, and three-quarters of an hour in thinking over what you have read.

THE GUIDE TO DAILY READING

PREPARED BY ASA DON DICKINSON

The elaborate, systematic "course of reading" is a bore. After thirty years spent among books and bookish people I have never yet met anyone who would admit that he had ploughed through such a course from beginning to end. Of course a few faithful souls, with abundant leisure, have done this, just as there are men who have walked from New York City to San Francisco. Good exercise, doubtless! But most of us have not time for feats of such questionable utility.

Yet I myself and most of the booklovers whom I know have started at one time or another to pursue a course of reading, and we have never regretted our attempts. Why? Because this is an excellent way to discover the comparatively small number of authors who have a message that we need to hear. When such an one is discovered, one may with a good conscience let the systematic course go by the board until one has absorbed all that is useful from the store of good things offered by the valuable new acquaintance.

Each one has his idiosyncrasies. If I may be permitted to allude to a personal failing, let me confess that I have never read "Paradise Lost" or "Pilgrim's Progress." I have hopefully dipped into them repeatedly, but--I don't like them. Some day I hope to, but until my mind is ready for these two great world-books, I do not intend to waste time by driving through them with set teeth. There are too many other good books that I do enjoy reading. "In brief, Sir, study what you most affect."

The "Guide to Daily Readings" which follows makes no claim to be systematic. The aim has been simply to introduce the reader to a goodly company of authors--to provide a daily flower of thought for the buttonhole, to-day a glorious rose of poetic fancy, to-morrow a pert little pansy of quaint humor.

Yet nearly all the selections are doubly significant and interesting if read upon the days to which they are especially assigned. For example, on New Year's Day it is suggested that one set one's house in order by reading Franklin's "Rules of Conduct," Longfellow's "Psalm of Life," Bryant's "Thanatopsis," and Lowell's "To the Future"; on January 19th, Poe's Birthday, one is directed to an excellent sketch of Poe and to typical examples of his best work, "The Raven" and "The Cask of Amontillado"; and on October 31st, Hallowe'en, one is reminded of Burns's "Tam O'Shanter" and Irving's "Legend of Sleepy Hollow."

The references are explicit in each case, so that it is a matter of only a few seconds to find each one. For example, the reference to the "Cask of Amontillado" is 4-Pt. I =67-77; which means that this tale is ten pages long and will be found in

Part I of volume 4, at page 67.

Excepting volumes 10-15 (Poetry), two volumes are bound in one in this set, so it should be remembered that generally there are two pages numbered 67 in each book.

The daily selections can in most cases be read in from fifteen minutes to half an hour, and Dr. Eliot, President Emeritus of Harvard, has said that fifteen minutes a day devoted to good literature will give every man the essentials of a liberal education. If time can be found between breakfast and the work-hours for these few minutes of reading, one will receive more benefit than if it is done during the somnolent period which follows the day's work and dinner. It is a mistake, however, to read before breakfast. Eyes and stomach are too closely related to permit of this.

Happy is he who can read these books in company with a sympathetic companion. His enjoyment of the treasure they contain will be doubled.

One final hint--when reading for something besides pastime, get in the habit of referring when necessary to dictionary, encyclopedia, and atlas. If on the subway or a railway train, jot down a memorandum of the query on the flyleaf, and look up the answer at the first opportunity.

ASA DON DICKINSON.

There is no business, no avocation whatever, which will not permit a man, who has the inclination, to give a little time, every day, to study. --DANIEL

WYTTENBACH.

JANUARY 1ST TO 7TH

1st. I. Franklin's Rules of Conduct, 6-Pt. II: 86-101 II. Longfellow's Psalm of Life, 14:247-248 III. Bryant's Thanatopsis, 15:18-20 IV. Lowell's To the Future, 13:164-167

2nd. I. Arnold's Self Dependence, 14:273-274 II. Adams's Cold Wave of 32 B. C., 9-Pt. I:146 III. Thomas's Frost To-night, 12:343

3rd. TOMASSO SALVINI, b. 1 Ja. 1829; d. 1 Ja. 1916 I. Tomasso Salvini, 17-II:80-108

4th. I. Extracts from Thackeray's Book of Snobs, 1-Pt. I:3-37

5th. I. Ruskin's Venice, 1-Pt. II:73-88 II. St. Marks, 1-Pt. II:91-100

6th. I. Shakespeare's Blow, Blow Thou Winter Wind, 12:256-257 II. Messenger's A Winter Wish, 12:259-261 III. Emerson's The Snow Storm, 14:93-94 IV. Thackeray's Nil Nisi Bonum, I-Pt. I:130-143

7th. I. Adams's Ballad of the Thoughtless Waiter, 9-Pt. I:147 II. Us Poets, 9-Pt. I:148 III. Spenser's Amoretti, 13:177

No book that will not improve by repeated readings deserves to be read at all. --THOMAS CARLYLE.

JANUARY 8TH TO 14th

8th. I. Fred Trover's Little Iron-clad, 7-Pt. II:82-105

9th. I. Kipling's The Man Who Would Be King, 21-Pt. II:1-56

10th. I. Carlyle's Boswell's Life of Johnson, 2-Pt. I: 32-78

11th. I ALEXANDER HAMILTON, b. II Ja. 1757 Alexander Hamilton, 16-Pt. I:71-91

12th. I. Macaulay's Dr. Samuel Johnson, His Biographer, 2-Pt. II:30-39 II. The Puritans, 2-Pt. II:23-29

13th. I. EDMUND SPENSER, d, 16 Ja. 1599 Prothalamion, 13:13-20

14th. I. Hawthorne's Dr. Heidegger's Experiment, 3-Pt. I:3-19

The novel, in its best form, I regard as one of the most powerful engines of civilization ever invented. --SIR JOHN HERSCHEL.

JANUARY 15TH TO 21ST

15th. EDWARD EVERETT, d. 15 Ja. 1865 I. Lincoln to Everett, 5-Pt. I:120 II. Irving's Westminster Abbey, 3-Pt. II:75-92

16th. GEORGE V. HOBART, b. 16 Ja. 1867 I. John Henry at the Races, 9-Pt. II:107-113 II. Poe's The Black Cat, 4-Pt. I:127-143

17th. BENJAMIN FRANKLIN, b. 17 Ja. 1706 I. Poor Richard's Almanac, 6-Pt. II:133-149 II. Maxims, 7-Pt. II:11 III. The Whistle, 6-Pt. II:156-159

18th. DANIEL WEBSTER, b. 18 Ja. 1782 I. Adams and Jefferson, 6-Pt. I:3-60

19th. EDGAR ALLAN POE, b. 19 Ja. 1809 I. Cask of Amontillado, 4-Pt. I:67-77 II. The Raven, 10:285-292 III. Edgar Allan Poe, 17-Pt. I:28-37

20th. N. P. WILLIS, b. 20 Ja. 1806 I. Miss Albina McLush, 7-Pt. I:25-29 RICHARD LE GALLIENNE, b. 20 Ja. 1866 II. May Is Building Her House, 12:328

21st. JAMES STUART, Earl of Murray, killed 21 Ja. 1570 I. The Bonny Earl of Murray, 10:21-22 II. Lincoln's The Dred Scott Decision, 5-Pt. I:13-22 III. Fragment on Slavery, 5-Pt. I:11-12

He that revels in a well-chosen library has innumerable dishes, and all of admirable flavour. His taste is rendered so acute as easily to distinguish the nicest shade of difference. --WILLIAM GODWIN.

JANUARY 22ND TO 28TH

22nd. LORD BYRON, b. 22 Ja. 1788 I. Macaulay's Lord Byron the Man, 2-Pt. II: 80-94 II. On This Day I Complete My Thirty-Sixth Year, 12:275-277 III. The Isles of Greece, 14:75-79

23rd. I. Lamb's Dream Children, 5-Pt. II:34-40 II. On Some of the Old Actors, 5-Pt. II:52-76

24th. I. Spenser's Epithalamium, 13:20-37

25th. ROBERT BURNS, b. 25 Ja. 1759 I. The Cotter's Saturday Night, II:40-48 II. Robert Burns, 17-Pt. 1:43-64 II. Halleck's Burns, 15:67-73

26th. THOMAS LOVELL BEDDOES, d. 26 Ja. 1849 I. Wolfram's Dirge, 15:42-43 II. How Many Times Do I Love Thee, Dear? 12:158-159 III. Dream-Pedlary, 12:227-228 IV. Franklin's Philosophical Experiments, 6-Pt. II:125-130

27th. JOHN McCRAE, Died in France 28 Ja. 1918 I. In Flanders Fields, 15:214

28th. HENRY MORTON STANLEY, b. 28 Ja. 1841 I. Henry Morton Stanley, 17-Pt. II:97-124

We enter our studies, and enjoy a society which we alone can bring together. We raise no jealousy by conversing with one in preference to another; we give no offence to the most illustrious by questioning him as long as we will, and leaving him as abruptly.... --WALTER SAVAGE LANDOR.

JANUARY 29TH TO FEBRUARY 4th

29th. ADELAIDE RISTORI, b. 30 Ja. 1822 I. Adelaide Ristori, 17-Pt. II:109-119 II. Thackeray's On Being Found Out, 1-Pt. I:104-115

30th. WALTER SAVAGE LANDOR, b. 30 Ja. 1775 I. Rose Aylmer,15:119 II. The Maid's Lament, 15:119-120 III. Mother I Cannot Mind My Wheel, 12:273 IV. On His Seventy-fifth Birthday, 13:278 V. Ruskin's The Two Boyhoods, 1-Pt. II:3-23

31st. I. Carlyle's Essay on Biography, 2-Pt. I:3-3l

F.1st. I. Morris's February,14:102-103 II. Belloc's South Country,12:331 III. Early Morning, 13:294

2nd. W.R.BENET, b. 2 F. 1886 I. Tricksters, 13:288 II. Hodgson's Eve, 11:324 III. The Gypsy Girl, 14:299

3rd. SIDNEY LANIER, b. 3 F. 1842 I. The Marshes of Glynn, 14:55-61 II. A Ballad of Trees and the Master, 12:316-317 III. The Stirrup Cup, 13:283

4th. THOMAS CARLYLE, d. 4 F. 1881 81 I. Mirabeau, 2-Pt. I:79-86 II. Ghosts, 2-Pt. I:134-137 III. Labor, 2-Pt. I:138-145

Borrow therefore, of those golden morning hours, and bestow them on your book. --EARL OF BEDFORD

FEBRUARY 5TH TO 11TH

5th. I. De Quincey's On the Knocking at the Gate In Macbeth, 4-Pt. II:100-107

6th. SIR HENRY IRVING, b. 6 F. 1838 I. Sir Henry Irving, 17-II:39-47

7th. CHARLES DICKENS, b. 7 F. 1812 I. The Trial for Murder, 21-Pt. I:1-19

8th. JOHN RUSKIN, b. 8 F. 1819 I. The Slave Ship, 1-Pt. II:27-29 II. Art and Morals, 1-Pt. II:103-132 III. Peace, 1-Pt. II:135-137

9th. GEORGE ADE, b. 9 F. 1866 I. The Fable of the Preacher, 9-Pt. II:67-71 II. The Fable of the Caddy, 9-Pt. II:93-94 III. The Fable of the Two Mandolin Players, 9-Pt. II:13I-136

10th. SIR JOHN SUCKLING, baptized 10 F. 1609 I. Encouragements to a Lover, 13:122 II. Constancy, 12:122-123 E. W. TOWNSEND, b. 10 F. 1855 III. Chimmie Meets the Duchess, 9-Pt. I 109-114

11th. I. Brooke's Dust, 12:341 II. 1914--V--The Soldier, 15: 228 III. Guiterman's In the Hospital, 15:203

The scholar, only, knows how dear these silent, yet eloquent, companions of pure thoughts and innocent hours become in the season of adversity. When all that is worldly turns to dross around us, these only retain their steady value. --Washington Irving.

February 12th to 18th

12th. Abraham Lincoln, b. 12 F. 1809 I. Lincoln, 16-Pt. I:93-141

13th. I. Irving's The Stout Gentleman, 3-Pt. II: 129-145

14th. W. T. Sherman, d. 14 F. 1891 I. General William Tecumseh Sherman, 16-Pt. II:32-61

15th. Charles Bertrand Lewis ("M. Quad") b. 15 F. 1842 I. The Patent Gas Regulator, 9-Pt. II:3-7 II. Two Cases of Grip, 8-Pt. I:50-53

16th. Joseph Hergesheimer, b. 15 F. 1880 I. A Sprig of Lemon Verbena, 22-Pt. II:1-47

17th. Josephine Dodge Daskam, b. 17 F. 1876 I. The Woman Who Was Not Athletic, 9-Pt. II:78-80 II. The Woman Who Used Her Theory, 9-Pt. II: 80-81 III. The Woman Who Helped Her Sister, 9-Pt. II:81-82

18th. I. De Quincey's The Affliction of Childhood, 4-Pt. II:3-30

What a place to be in is an old library! It seems though all the souls of all the writers were reposing here. --CHARLES LAMB.

FEBRUARY 19TH TO 25th

19th. I. Conrad's The Lagoon, 22-Pt. I:17-37

20th. JOSEPH JEFFERSON, b. 20 F. 1829 I. Joseph Jefferson, 17-Pt. II:3-22

21st. JOHN HENRY NEWMAN, b. 21 F. 1801 I. The Pillar of the Cloud, 12:323 II. Sensitiveness, 15:183-184 III. Flowers Without Fruit, 15:184 IV. Lincoln's Address at Cooper Institute, 5-Pt. I:37-69

22nd. GEORGE WASHINGTON, b. 22 F. 1732 I. Washington, 16-Pt. I:3-42

23rd. I. Mrs. Freeman's The Wind in the Rosebush, 20-Pt. II:12-38

24th. SAMUEL LOVER, b. 24 F. 1797 I. The Gridiron, 19-Pt. II:59-70

25th. I. Lamb's Superannuated Man, 5-Pt. II: 80-91 II. Old China, 5-Pt. II:91-100

A little peaceful home Sounds all my wants and wishes; add to this My book and friend, and this is happiness. --FRANCESCO DI RIOJA.

FEBRUARY 26TH TO MARCH 4TH

26th. SAM WALTER FOSS, d. 26 F. 1911 I. The Prayer of Cyrus Brown, 9-Pt. II:8 II. The Meeting of the Clabberhuses, 8-Pt. I: 39-41 III. A Modern Martyrdom, 9-Pt. II: 84-86 IV. The Ideal Husband to His Wife, 9-Pt. I:103-104

27th. HENRY WADSWORTH LONGFELLOW, b. 27 F. 1807 I. Henry Wadsworth Longfellow, 17-Pt. I:3-27 II. Wreck of the Hesperus, 10:156-160 III. My Lost Youth, 12:263-266

28th. ELLEN TERRY, b. 27 F. 1848 I. Ellen Terry, 17-Pt. II:48-60

Mr.1st I. Morris's March, 14:103-104 W. D. HOWELLS, b. 1 Mr. 1837 II. Mrs. Johnson, 8-Pt. II:107-128

2nd. I. Franklin's Settling Down, 6-Pt. II:76-85 II. Public Affairs, 6-Pt. II:102-107

3rd. EDMUND WALLER, b. 9 Mr. 1606 I. On a Girdle, 12:132 II. Go, Lovely Rose, 12:136-137 III. De la Mare's The Listeners, 11:327

4th. Inauguration Day I. Lincoln's First Inaugural Address, 5-Pt. I:74-89

A little library, growing larger every year, is an honorable part of a man's history. It is a man's duty to have books. A library is not a luxury, but one of the necessaries of life. --HENRY WARD BEECHER.

MARCH 5TH TO 11TH

5th. FRANK NORRIS, b. 5 Mr. 1870 I. The Passing of Cock-Eye Blacklock, 22-Pt. II:64

6th. ELIZABETH BARRETT BROWNING, b. 6 Mr. 1806 I. Mother and Poet, 11:297-302 II. A Musical Instrument, 12: 282-283 III. The Cry of the Children,

12: 296-302

7th. I. Thackeray's On a Lazy Idle Boy, 1-Pt. I: 41-51

8th. HENRY WARD BEECHER, d. 8 Mr. 1887 I. Deacon Marble, 7-Pt. I:13-15 II. The Deacon's Trout, 7-Pt. I:15-16 III. Noble and the Empty Hole, 7-Pt. I:17-18

9th. ANNA LETITIA BARBAULD, d. 9 Mr. 1825 I. Life, 14:260-261 II. Dunsany's Night at an Inn, 18:I

10th. I. Ruskin's The Mountain Gloom, 1-Pt. II: 33-56

11th. CHARLES SUMNER, d. n Mr. 1874 I. Longfellow's Charles Sumner, 15:111-112 GILES FLETCHER, buried 11 Mr. 1611 II. Wooing Song, 12:101-102 III. Carlyle's Reward, 2-Pt. I:146-160

Books that can be held in the hand, and carried to the fireside are the best after all. --SAMUEL JOHNSON.

MARCH 12TH TO 18TH

12th. I. A Family Horse, 9-Pt. I:3-14 II. Living in the Country, 7-Pt. I:82-95

13th. I. Macaulay's Task of the Modern Historian, 2-Pt. II:3-22 II. Puritans, 2-Pt. II:23-29

14th. HENRY IV. defeated the "Leaguers" at Ivry, 14 Mr. 1590 I. Macaulay's Ivry, 10:194-199

15th. JOHANN LUDWIG PAUL HEYSE, b. 15 Mr. 1830 I. L'Arrabiata, 20-Pt. I:130-157

16th. WILL IRWIN, b. 15 Mr. 1876 I. The Servant Problem, 7-Pt. I:132

17th. I. Hawthorne's The Great Stone Face, 3-Pt. I:103-135

18th. I. Roche's The V-A-S-E, 7-Pt. II:60-61 II. Roche's A Boston Lullaby, 8-Pt. II:78 III. A Boston Lullaby (Anon.), 7-Pt. II:105 IV. Burgess's The Bohemians of Boston, 7-Pt. II:141-143

The first time I read an excellent book, it is to me just as if I had gained a new friend; when I read over a book I have perused before, it resembles the meeting with an old one. --OLIVER GOLDSMITH.

MARCH 19TH TO 25th

19th. THOMAS BAILEY ALDRICH, d. 19 Mr. 1907 I. A Rivermouth Romance, 7-Pt. II:129-140 II. A Death Bed, 15:136-137

20th. CHARLES GODFREY LELAND, d. 20 Mr. 1903 I. Ballad, 7-Pt. II:51-52 II. Hans Breitmann's Party, 7-Pt. I:96-97 III. De Quincey's Levana, 4-Pt. II:145-157

21st. ROBERT SOUTHEY, d. 21 Mr. 1843 I. The Inchcape Rock, 10:153-156 II. My Days Among the Dead Are Past, 14: 261-262 III. Lincoln's Springfield Speech, 5-Pt. I:23-36

22nd. I. Lamb's Two Races of Men, 5-Pt. II:3-11

23rd. JOHN DAVIDSQN, disappeared 23 Mr. 1909 I. Butterflies, 12:345 II. Doyle's Dancing Men, 22-Pt. I:63-l00

24th. HENRY WADSWORTH LONGFELLOW, d. 24 Mr. 1882 I. The Building of the Ship, II:89-102 II. The Skeleton in Armor, 10:124-130 III. Resignation, 15:131-133 IV. The Arrow and the Song, 12:283-284

25th. I. Franklin's George Whitefield, 6-Pt. II: 108-114 II. The Franklin Stove, 6-Pt. II:115-116 III. Civic Pride, 6-Pt. II:117-124 IV. Advice to a Young Tradesman, 6-Pt. II: 153-155

For whatsoever things were written aforetime were written for our learnings. --ST. PAUL.

MARCH 26TH TO APRIL 1ST

26th. A. E. HOUSMAN, b. 26 Mr. 1859 I. A Shropshire Lad-XIII, 12:340 II. Ferber's Gay Old Dog, 22-Pt. II:81-114

27th. I. Thackeray's Thorns in the Cushion, 1-Pt. I:51-64

28th. FOCH, made Commander Allied Armies, 28 Mr. 1918 I. Burr's Fall In, 15:211 II. Coates's Place de la Concorde, 15:226

29th. BONNIVARD, Prisoner of Chillon, liberated 29 Mr. 1536 I. Byron's Prisoner of Chillon, 11:191-204

30th. DE WOLF HOPPER, b. 30 Mr. 1858 I. Casey at the Bat, 9-Pt. I:95-98 II. Butler's Just Like a Cat, 8-Pt. I:152

31st. ANDREW MARVELL, b,. 31 Mr. 1621 I. The Garden, 14:20-22 II. Bermudas, 15:162-163 JOHN DONNE, d. 31 Mr. 1631 III. The Dream, 12:137-138 IV. The Will, 15:156-158 V. Death, 13:195-196 VI. A Burnt Ship, 13:272

Ap. 1st. AGNES REPPLIER, b. 1 Ap. 1858 I. A Plea for Humor, 8-Pt. II:3-25

Dreams, books are each a world; and books, we know, Are a substantial world, both pure and good: Round these, with tendrils, strong as flesh and blood, Our pastime and our happiness will grow. --WILLIAM WORDSWORTH.

APRIL 2ND TO 8TH

2nd. I. Jefferson, 16-Pt. I:43-70 Nelson's Victory Over the Danish Fleet, 2 Ap. 1801 II. The Battle of the Baltic, 10:189-192

3rd. WASHINGTON IRVING, b. 3 Ap. 1783 I. Wouter Van Twiller, 7-Pt. I:3-10 II. The Voyage, 3-Pt. II:61-71

4th. I. Browning's Home Thoughts from Abroad, 12:57-58 II. Macaulay's Byron the Poet, 2-Pt. II:94-109

5th. FRANK R. STOCKTON, b. 5 Ap. 1834 I. Pomona's Novel, 7-Pt. II:62-81 II. A Piece of Red Calico, 8-Pt. I:105-112

6th. COMMANDER ROBERT E. PEARY reached the North Pole, 6 Ap. 1909 I. At the North Pole, 16-Pt. II:125-151

7th. WILLIAM WORDSWORTH, b. 7 Ap. 1770 I. Landor's To Wordsworth, 14:148-150 II. To the Cuckoo, 12:38-40 III. Daffodils, 12:41-42 IV. Tintern Abbey, 14:47-52 V. Lucy Gray, 10:255-258 VI. Arnold's Memorial Verses, 15:77-79

8th. PHINEAS FLETCHER, baptized, 8 Ap. 1582 I. A Hymn, 12:317 ROBERT HAVEN SCHAUFFLER, b. 8 Ap.1879 II. Earth's Easter (1915), 15:224 III. Hagedorn's Song Is So Old, 12:337

But words are things, and a small drop of ink, falling like dew, upon a thought, produces that which makes thousands, perhaps millions, think. -- LORD BYRON.

APRIL 9TH TO 15TH

9th. I. Tennyson's Early Spring, 14:94-96 II. Poe's Ligeia, 4-Pt. I:37-63

10th. I. De Quincey's The Vision of Sudden Death, 4-Pt. II:119-145

11th. NAPOLEON abdicated at Fontainebleau, 11 Ap. 1814 I. Byron's Ode to Napoleon Buonaparte, 13:109-115

12th. I. Franklin's Autobiography, 6-Pt. II:3-35

13th. I. Burns's To a Mountain Daisy, 14:109-111 II. Lamb's Imperfect Sympathies, 5-Pt. II:21-34

14th. LINCOLN shot by John Wilkes Booth, 14 Ap. 1865 I. Markham's, Lincoln the Man of the People, 14:296 II. Flecker's Dying Patriot, 10:295 III. Ballad of Camden Town, 12:347

15th. ABRAHAM LINCOLN, d. 15 Ap. 1865 I. Farewell at Springfield, 5-Pt. I:70 II. Speech to 166th Ohio Regiment, 5-Pt. I:96-97 III. Letters to Mrs. Lincoln, 5-Pt. I:113-114 IV. To Grant, 5-Pt. I:121 V. Whitman's O Captain! My Captain! 15:105-106 Titanic Sunk, 15 Ap. 1912 VI. Van Dyke's Heroes of the Titanic, 10:305

Many times the reading of a book has made the fortune of a man--has decided his way of life. --RALPH WALDO EMERSON.

APRIL 16TH TO 22ND

16th. I. Herbert's Easter, 15:152-153 II. Franklin's Motion for Prayers, 6-Pt. II: 62-164 III. Necessary Hints, 6-Pt. II: 160-161

17th. BENJAMIN FRANKLIN, d. 17 Ap. 1790 I. Franklin's Autobiography, 6-Pt. II:35-75 DR. CHARLES H. PARKHURST, b. 17 Ap. 1842 II. A Remarkable Dream, 8-Pt. I:79-80

18th. RICHARD HARDING DAVIS, b. 18 Ap. 1864 I. Mr. Travers's First Hunt, 22-Pt. I:135 II. A Slave to Duty, 8-Pt. I:66-67

19th. Battles of Lexington and Concord, 19 Ap. 1775 I. Emerson's Concord Hymn, 12:218-219 Siege of Ratisbon, 19-23 Ap. 1809 II. Browning's Incident of the French Camp, 10:213-214

20th. I. Campbell's Ye Mariners of England, 10: 150-151 II. Lincoln's Response to Serenade, 5-Pt. I: 98-100 WILLIAM H. DAVIS, b. 20 Ap. 1870 III. Davies's Catharine, 11:327

21st. CHARLOTTE BRONT? b. 21 Ap. 1816 I. Charlotte Bront? 17-Pt. I:121-132 II. Thackeray's De Juventute, 1-Pt. I:65-87

22nd. I. Riley's The Elf-Child, 8-Pt. I:34-36 II. A Liz-Town Humorist, 8-Pt. I:48-49 III. Carlyle's The Watch Tower, 2-Pt. I:129-133 UNITED STATES DAY CELEBRATED IN FRANCE 22 Ap. 1917 IV. Van Dyke's The Name of France, 15:224

Knowing I loved my books, he furnished me, From my own library, with volumes that I prize above my dukedom. --WILLIAM SHAKESPEARE.

APRIL 23RD TO 29TH

23rd. WILLIAM SHAKESPEARE, b. 23 (?) Ap. 1564; d/ 23 Ap. 1616 I. When Daises Pied, 12:18-19 II. Under the Greenwood Tree, 12:21 III. Hark, Hark, The Lark, 12:97 IV. Milton's Epitaph on Shakespeare, 15:44 V. Stratford-on-Avon, 3-Pt. II:151-181

24th. JAMES T. FIELDS, d. 24 Ap. 1881 I. The Owl-Critic, 7-Pt. I: 41-44 II. The Alarmed Skipper, 7-Pt. I:75-76 LORD DUNSANY, wounded 25 Ap. 1916 III. Songs from an Evil Wood, 15:221

25th. OLIVER CROMWELL, b. 25 Ap. 1599 I. Marvell's Upon Cromwell's Return from Ireland, 13:54-59 II. To the Lord General Cromwell, 13:201-202 JOHN KEBLE, b. 25 Ap. 1792 III. Morning, 15:173-175 IV. Evening, 15:175-177

26th. CHARLES FARRAR BROWNE (Artemus Ward,) b. 26 Ap. 1834 I. One of Mr. Ward's Business Letters, 8-Pt. II:68-69 II. On Forts, 8-Pt. II:69-71 III. Among the Spirits, 8-Pt. I:81-85

27th. U. S. GRANT, b. 27 Ap. 1822 I. General Ulysses Simpson Grant, 16--Pt. II: 3-30

28th. 28 Ap. 1864 "Tell Tad the Goats are Well." I. Lincoln's Telegram to Mrs. Lincoln, 5--Pt. I:114 II. The Last Address in Public, April 11, 1865, 5--Pt. I:102-106

29th. E. R. SILL, b. 29 Ap. 1841 I. Five Lives, 7--Pt. I:39-40 II. Eve's Daughter, 9--Pt. I:102 III. Opportunity, 11:106 IV. The Fool's Prayer, 11:263-264.

I own that I am disposed to say grace upon twenty other occasions in the course of the day besides my dinner....Why have we none for books? -- CHARLES LAMB.

APRIL 30th TO MAY 6TH

April 30th. I. Peck's Bessie Brown, M. D., 8-Pt. II:81-82 II. A Kiss in the Rain, 9-Pt. II:83 III. Poe's Fall of the House of Usher, 4-Pt. I:3-34

May 1st. I. Morris's May, 14:104-105 Battle of Manila Bay, I My. 1898 II. Ware's Manila, 8-Pt. I:173 S.S. Lusitania torpedoed I My. 1916 III. Graves's It's a Queer Time, 15:219 HARRY LEON WILSON, b. I My. 1867 IV. Ruggles and Fate, 22-Pt. II:115

2nd. I. Lowell's To the Dandelion, 14:116-118 II. Lamb's Farewell to Tobacco, 5-Pt. II:149-154 III. She Is Going, 5-Pt. II:154

3rd. I. Browning's Two in the Campagna, 14:187-189 II. Franklin's Letters, 6-Pt. II:167-178

4th. RICHARD HOVEY, b. 4 My. 1864 I. The Sea Gypsy, 12:334 II. Braithwaite's Sic Vita, 12:343 III. Sandy Star, 12:346

5th. CHRISTOPHER MORLEY, b. 5 My. 1890 I. Rhubarb, 22-Pt. II:56

6th. ABB?VOGLER, d. 6 My. 1814 I. Abt Vogler, 14:177-183 ROBERT EDWIN PEARY, b. 6 My. 1857 II. Robert E. Peary, 16-Pt. II:125-146

Where a book raises your spirit, and inspires you with noble and courageous feelings, seek for no other rule to judge the event by: it is good and made by a good workman. --JEAN BE LA BRUY 萊 E.

MAY 7TH TO 13TH

7th. ROBERT BROWNING, b. 7 My. 1812 I. Landor's To Robert Browning, 14:151-152 II. A King Lived Long Ago, 11:9-11 III. Evelyn Hope, 15:121-123 IV. How They Brought the Good News, 10:130-134 V. A Woman's Last Word, 14:189-191

8th. I. Shakespeare's Sonnets, 13:184-195 II. Peabody's Fortune and Men's Eyes, 18:89

9th. J. M. BARRIE, b. 9 My. 1860 I. The Courting of T'Nowhead's Bell, 20-Pt. I:1-29

10th. HENRY M. STANLEY, d. 10 My. 1904 I. In Darkest Africa, 16-Pt. II:97-124

11th. I. Wordsworth's The Green Linnet, 14:106-108 GEORGE EDWARD WOODBERRY, b. 12 My. 1855 II. At Gibraltar, 13:290

12th. DANTE GABRIEL ROSSETTI, b. 12 My. 1828 I. The Blessed Damozel, 10:58-63 II. The Sonnet, 13:176-177 III. The House of Life, 13:257-264

13th. ALPHONSE DAUDET, b. 13 My. 1840 I. The Siege of Berlin, 21-Pt. I:129-138

Learn to be good readers--which is perhaps a more difficult thing than you imagine. Learn to be discriminative in your reading; to read faithfully, and with your best attention, all kinds of things which you have a real interest in. --THOMAS CARLYLE.

MAY 14TH TO 20TH

14th. "Mother's Day" (2d Sunday in May) I. Branch's Songs for My Mother, 14:300 II. Emerson's Each and All, 14:262-263 III. Carlyle's Battle of Dunbar, 2-Pt. I:142-159

15th. I. Thackeray's On Letts's Diary, 1-Pt. I:115-130

16th. HONOR?DE BALZAC, b. 20 My. 1799 I. A Passion in the Desert, 21-Pt. II:107-129

17th. I. Thackeray's On a Joke I Once Heard, I-Pt. I:89-104

18th. I. Browning's May and Death, 15:123-124 II. Galsworthy's The Little Man, 18:227

19th. Battle of La Hogue 19 My. 1692 (N. S. 29 My. 1692) I. Browning's Herv?Riel, 10:162-168 NATHANIEL HAWTHORNE, d. 19 My. 1864 II. The Great Carbuncle, 20-Pt. II:30-52

20th. I. Gerstenberg's Overtones, 18:139

At this day, as much company as I have kept, and as much as I love it, I love reading better. --ALEXANDER POPE.

MAY 21ST TO 27TH

21st. ALEXANDER POPE, b. 21 My. 1688 I. On a Certain Lady at Court, 13:272-273 II. The Dying Christian to His Soul, 15:169 III. The Universal Prayer,

15:166-168 JAMES GRAHAM, Marquis of Montrose, d. 21 My. 1650 IV. The Execution of Montrose, 10:270-277

22nd. ARTHUR CONAN DOYLE, b. 22 My. 1859 I. The Dancing Men, 22-Pt. I:63

23rd. THOMAS HOOD, b. 23 My. 1799 I. Flowers, 12:53-54 II. I Remember, I Remember, 12:269-270 III. The Song of the Shirt, 12:292-295 IV. The Bridge of Sighs, 15:124-128 V. The Dream of Eugene Aram, 11:265-273

24th. RICHARD MANSFIELD, b. 24 My. 1857 I. Richard Mansfield, 17-Pt. II:61-79

25th. RALPH WALDO EMERSON, b. 25 My. 1803 I. The Rhodora, 14:115 II. The Titmouse, 12:66-69 III. The Problem, 14:268-271 IV. Lincoln's The Whigs and the Mexican War, 5-Pt. I:3-6 V. Notes for a Law Lecture, 5-Pt. I:7-10

26th. I. Bret Harte's Melons, 7-Pt. II:41-50 II. The Society upon the Stanislaus, 7-Pt. II:57-59

27th. I. Lady Dufferin's The Lament of the Irish Emigrant, 15:128-130 II. Hawthorne's Wakefield, 3-Pt. I:85-99

All the best experience of humanity, folded, saved, freighted to us here! Some of these tiny ships we call Old and New Testaments, Homer, Aeschylus, Plato, Juvenal, etc. Precious Minims! --WALT WHITMAN.

MAY 28TH TO JUNE 3RD

28th. THOMAS MOORE, b. 28 My. 1779 I. As Slow Our Ship, 12:232-233 II. Believe Me If All Those Endearing Young Charms, 12:157-158 III. The Lake of the Dismal Swamp, 11:83-85 IV. Oft in the Stilly Night, 12:271-272 V. Fly to the Desert, 12:155-157 VI. Canadian Boat Song, 12:233-234

29th I. De Quincey's Pleasures of Opium, 4-Pt. II:31-73

30th. Memorial Day I. Hale's The Man Without a Country, 21-Pt. II:57-95

31st. WALT WHITMAN, b. 31 My. 1819 I. Out of the Cradle Endlessly Rocking, 14: 120-129

Je. 1st. HENRY FRANCIS LYTE, b. 1 Je. 1793 I. Abide With Me, 15:180-181 JOHN DRINKWATER, b. 1 Je. 1882 II. Birthright, 15:199 CHRISTOPHER MARLOWE, killed in a street brawl, 1 Je. 1593 III. Porcelain Cups, 22-Pt. I:38-62

2nd. J. G. SAXE, b. 2 Je. 1816 I. Early Rising II. The Coquette III. The Stammering Wife IV. My Familiar, THOMAS HARDY, b. 2 Je. 1840 V. Hardy's The Oxen, 15:201

3rd. I. Hood's It Was Not in the Winter, II. Lamb's Letters,

We ought to regard books as we do sweetmeats, not wholly to aim at the pleasantest, but chiefly to respect the wholesomest; not forbidding either, but approving the latter most. --PLUTARCH.

JUNE 4TH TO 10th

4th. I. Thackeray's Dennis Haggarty's Wife, 21-Pt. I:20-52

5th. O. HENRY, d. 5 Je. 1910 I. The Furnished Room, 22-Pt. I:140

6th. ROBERT FALCON SCOTT, b. 6 Je. 1868 I. Captain Scott's Last Struggle, 16-Pt. II: 152-159

7th. EDWIN BOOTH, d. 7 Je. 1893 I. Edwin Booth, 17-Pt. II:23-38

8th. I. Lamb's Letters, 5-Pt. II:103-106

9th. CHARLES DICKENS, d. 9 Je. 1870 I. Charles Dickens, 17-Pt. I:99-120

10th. EDWARD EVERETT HALE, d. 10 Je. 1909 I. My Double and How He Undid Me, 8-Pt. I:124-142

If an author be worthy of anything, he is worth bottoming. It may be all very well to skim milk, for the cream lies on the top; but who could skim Lord Byron? --GEORGE SEARLE PHILLIPS.

JUNE 11TH TO 17TH

11th. I. Wells's Tragedy of a Theatre Hat, 9-Pt. II:50-55 II. One Week,9-Pt. II:151 III. The Poster Girl, 8-Pt. II:92-93 IV. A Memory, 9-Pt. I:116-117

12th. CHARLES KINGSLEY, b. 12 Je. 1819 I. Oh! That We Two Were Maying, 12:175-176 II. The Last Buccaneer, 14:240-242 III. The Sands of Dee, 10:261-262 IV. The Three Fishers, 10:262-263 V. Lorraine, 11:306-308

13th. WILLIAM BUTLER YEATS, b. 13 Je. 1865 I. Ballad of Father Gilligan, 10:314 II. Fiddler of Dooney, 14:310

14th. Flag Day I. Whittier's Barbara Frietchie, 10:210-213 II. Key's Star-Spangled Banner, 12:213-215 III. Drake's American Flag, 12:215-217 IV. Holmes's Old Ironsides, 12:217-218

15th. I. Leacock's My Financial Career, 9-Pt. II:19-23 II. Hawthorne's Gray Champion, 3-Pt. I:139-152

16th. I. Lanigan's The Villager and the Snake, 9-Pt-I:19 II. The Amateur Orlando, 9-Pt. I:26-30 III. The Ahkoond of Swat, 8-Pt. I: 37-38

17th. JOSEPH ADDISON, d. 17 Je. 1719 I. The Voice of the Heavens, 15:165-166 II. Poe's MS. Found in a Bottle, 4-Pt. I:105-123 III. Lincoln's Emancipation

Proclamation, 5-Pt. I:90-93 IV. Ship of State and Pilot, 5-Pt. I:94-95

Sitting last winter among my books, and walled around with all the comfort and protection which they and my fireside could afford me--to wit, a table of higher piled books at my back, my writing desk on one side of me, some shelves on the other, and the feeling of the warm fire at my feet--I began to consider how I loved the authors of those books. --LEIGH HUNT.

JUNE 18th TO 24TH

18th. I. Hawthorne's Ethan Brand, 3-Pt. I:55-82

19th. RICHARD MONCKTON MILNES, d. Aug. 11, 1885 I. The Brook-Side, 12:177-178 II. The Men of Old, 14:133-135 III. Lincoln's Speech in Independence Hall, 5-Pt. I:71-73 IV. To the Workingmen of Manchester, 5-Pt. I:115-117

20th. I. Longfellow's Hymn to the Night, 12:46-47 II. The Light of the Stars, 12:48-49 III. Daybreak, 12:49-50 IV. Seaweed, 14:88-89 V. The Village Blacksmith, 14:165-166

21st. HENRY GUY CARLETON, b. 21 Je. 1856 I. The Thompson Street Poker Club, 7-Pt. II: 116-121 II. Munkittrick's Patriotic Tourist, 9-Pt. II: 47-48 III. What's in a Name, 9-Pt. II:103-104 IV. 'Tis Ever Thus, 9-Pt. II:152

22nd. ALAN SEEGER, b. 22 Je. 1888 I. I Have a Rendezvous with Death, 15:215 II. O. Henry's Gift of the Magi, 22-Pt. II:48

23rd. I. Longfellow's The Day Is Done, 12:240-242. II. The Beleaguered City, 14:249-251 III. The Bridge, 12:279-282 IV. Whittier's Ichabod, 14:154-156 V. Maud Muller, 11:219-224

24th. AMBROSE BIERCE, b. 24 Je. 1842 I. The Dog and the Bees, 7-Pt. II:10 II. The Man and the Goose, 9-Pt. I:85 Battle of Bannockburn, 24 Je. 1314 III.

Burns's Bannockburn, 12:198-199 IV. My Heart's in the Highlands, 12:36-37 V. The Banks of Doon, 12:146-147

Next to the originator of a good sentence is the first quoter of it. Many will read the book before one thinks of quoting a passage. As soon as he has done this, that line will be quoted east and west. --RALPH WALDO EMERSON.

JUNE 25TH TO JULY 1ST

25th. I. Goodman's Eugenically Speaking, 18:193

26th. I. Burns's Elegy, 15:61-64 II. Mary Morison, 12: 147-148 III. Oh! Saw Ye Bonnie Lesley? 12:148-149 IV. O, My Love's Like a Red, Red Rose, 12:149-150 V. Ae Fond Kiss, 12:150-151

27th. HELEN KELLER, b. 27 Je. 1880 I. Helen Keller, 17-Pt. I:167-171 II. Garrison's A Love Song, 12:338

28th. I. Lincoln's Letter to Bryant, 5--Pt. I:122-123 II. Burns's Of A' the Airts, 12:151 III. Highland Mary, 12:152-153 IV. A Farewell, 12:199-200 V. It Was A' for Our Rightfu' King, 12:200-201

29th. I. The Pit and the Pendulum, 21-Pt. I:139-162

30th. I. Burns's John Anderson My Jo, 12:245-246 II. Thou Lingering Star, 12:270-271 III. Lines Written on a Banknote, 13:273-274 IV. Byron's Darkness, 11:102-105 V. Oh! Snatch'd Away in Beauty's Bloom, 15:113-114

Jl. 1st. HARRIET BEECHER STOWE, d. 1 Jl. 1896 I. The Minister's Wooing, 8-Pt. II:97-106

A library is not worth anything without a catalogue; it is a Polyphemus without an eye in his head--and you must confront the difficulties whatever they may be, of making a proper catalogue. --Thomas Carlyle.

July 2nd to 8th

2nd. Richard Henry Stoddard, b. 2 Jl. 1825 I. There Are Gains for All Our Losses, 12:267 II. The Sky, 13:281 III. Byron's Ode on Venice, 13:115-121 IV. Stanzas for Music, 12:162-163 V. When We Two Parted, 12: 163-164

3rd. Charlotte Perkins (Stetson) Oilman, b. 3 Jl. 1860 I. Similar Cases, 9-Pt. I:53-57 II. Byron's She Walks in Beauty, 12:164-165 III. Destruction of Sennacherib, 11:183-184 IV. Sonnet on Chillon, 13:222

4th. Nathaniel Hawthorne, b. 4 Jl. 1804 I. Nathaniel Hawthorne, 17-Pt. I.74-98 Declaration of Independence, 4 Jl. 1776 II. Emerson's Ode, 13:167-169

5th. I. Emerson's Waldeinsamkeit, 14:39-41 II. The World Soul, 12:59-63 III. To the Humblebee, 12:64-66 IV. The Forerunners, 14:265-267 V. Brahma, 14:271

6th. I. Macdonald's Earl o' Quarterdeck, 10:300

7th. I. Markham's Man with the Hoe, 14:294

8th. Shelley drowned, 8 Jl. 1822 I. Memorabilia, 14:151 II. Hawthorne's The Minister's Black Veil, 21-Pt. I:107-128

For my part I have ever gained the most profit, and the most pleasure also, from the books which have made me think the most. --JULIUS C. HARE.

JULY 9TH TO 15TH

9th. I. Browning's The Statue and the Bust, II: 273-284 II. The Lost Leader, 12:289-290 III. The Patriot, II:290-291

10th. ALBERT BIGELOW PAINE, b. 10 Jl. 1861 I. Mis' Smith, 8-Pt. II:77 F. P.

DUNNE, ("Mr. Dooley"), b. 10 Jl. 1867 II. Home Life of Geniuses, 9-Pt. II:56-62 III. The City as a Summer Resort, 9-Pt. II:138-144

11th. I. Burdette's Vacation of Mustapha, 8-Pt. I:3-7 II. The Legend of Mimir, 8-Pt. I:68-69 III. The Artless Prattle of Childhood, 7-Pt. II. 106-112 IV. Rheumatism Movement Cure, 8-Pt. II:37-43

12th. B. P. SHILLABER, b. 12 Jl. 1814 I. Fancy Diseases, 7-Pt. I:32 II. Bailed Out, 7-Pt. I:33 III. Masson's My Subway Guard Friend, 9-Pt. I:140

13th. I. Mukerji's Judgment of Indra, 18:257

14th. The Bastille Destroyed, 14 Jl. 1789 I. Carlyle's The Flight to Varennes from "The French Revolution," 2-Pt. I:87-110

15th. Battle of Ch 鉳 eau Thierry, 15 Jl. 1918 I. Grenfell's Into Battle, 15:217 II. Keats's La Belle Dame Sans Merci, 10:85-87 III. Ode to a Nightingale, 13:132-135 IV. Ode, 13:135-137 V. Ode to Psyche, 13:139-141 VI. Fancy, 13:143-146

Books are the food of youth, the delight of old age; the ornament of prosperity; the refuge and comfort of adversity; a delight at home, and no hindrance abroad; companions at night, in travelling, in the country. --CICERO.

JULY 16TH TO 22ND

16th. ROALD AMUNDSEN, b. 16 Jl. 1872 I. Amundsen, 16-Pt. II:147-15l II. Masefield's Sea Fever, 12:334

17th. I. Keats's Robin Hood, 14: 146-148 II. Sonnets, 13:223-227 III. Shelley's Hymn of Pan, 12:44-45 IV. Lines Written Among the Euganean Hills, 14: 61-73 V. Stanzas Written in Dejection, 14:73-75

18th. WILLIAM MAKEPEACE THACKERAY, b. 18 Jl. 1811 I. De Finibus, 1-Pt.

I:143-157 II. Ballads, 1-Pt. I:161-164

19th. I. Derby's Illustrated Newspaper, 7-Pt. II: 11-19 II. Tushmaker's Toothpuller, 7-Pt. II:53-56 III. Burdette's Romance of the Carpet, 9-Pt. I: 38-40

20th. JEAN INGELOW, d.20 Jl.1897 I. High Tide on the Coast of Lincolnshire, 10:263-269 II. Shelley's The Cloud, 14:90-93 III. Hymn to Intellectual Beauty, 13:121-124 IV. To a Skylark, 13:124-129 V. Arethusa, 11:140-143

21st. Robert Burns, d. 21 Jl. 1796 I. Thoughts, 15:65-67 II. Shelley's Love's Philosophy, 12:160 III. I Fear Thy Kisses, 12:161 IV. To----, 12:161-162 V. To---, 12:162

22nd. I. Shelley's Ozymandias of Egypt, 13:222-223 II. Song, 12:225-226 III. When the Lamp Is Shattered, 12:274-275 IV. Tennyson's The Gardener's Daughter, II:17-28 V. The Deserted House, 15:23-24

Histories make men wise; poets, witty; the mathematics, subtile; natural philosophy, deep; morals, grave; logic and rhetoric, able to contend. --BACON.

July 23rd to 29th

23rd. U. S. Grant, d. 23 Jl. 1885 I. Lincoln to Grant, 5-Pt. I:121 II. Tennyson's Ulysses, 14:175-177 III. Ask Me No More, 12:180 IV. The Splendor Falls, 12:181 V. Come into the Garden, Maud, 12:182-184 VI. Sir Galahad, 14: 184-186

24th. John Newton, b. 24 Jl. 1725. I. The Quiet Heart, 15:170 II. Tennyson's The Miller's Daughter, II:31-40 III. The Oak, 14:41 IV. Sir Launcelot and Queen Guinevere, 10:51-53 V. Song, 12:54-55

25th. I. Tennyson's The Throstle, 12:55-56 II. A Small, Sweet Idyl, 14:79-80 III. Merlin and the Gleam, II:122-127 IV. The Lotos-Eaters, 14:135-143 V. Mariana, 14:162-164

26th. I. Stevenson's Markheim, 20-Pt. I:103-129

27th. Thomas Campbell, b. 27 Jl. 1777 I. The Soldier's Dream, 10:186-187 II. Lord Ullin's Daughter, 10:259-261 III. How Delicious Is the Winning, 12:165-166 IV. To the Evening Star, 12:47

28th. ABRAHAM COWLEY, d. 28 Jl. 1667 I. A Supplication, 13:59-60 II. On the Death of Mr. William Hervey, 15:80-86 JOHN GRAHAM OF CLAVERHOUSE VISCOUNT DUNDEE, d. 28 Jl. 1689 III. Scott's Bonny Dundee, 10:183-186

29th. DON MARQUIS, b. 29 Jl. 1878 I. Chant Royal of the Dejected Dipsomaniac, 9-Pt. I:143 BOOTH TARKINGTON, b. 29 Jl. 1869 II. Overwhelming Saturday, 22-Pt. I:101

Knowledge is proud that he has learned so much; Wisdom is humble that he knows no more. Books are not seldom talismans and spells. --COWPER.

July 30th to August 5th

30th. JOYCE KILMER, killed in action, 30 Jl. 1918 I. A Ballad of Three, 10:311 II. Trees, 12:329 III. Noyes's The May Tree, 12:327

31st. I. Tennyson's Song of the Brook, 14:99-101 II. O That 't Were Possible, 12:185-188 III. Morte d'Arthur, 11:204-215 IV. Sweet and Low, 12:249-250 V. Will, 14:259-260

Ag. 1st I. Tennyson's Rizpah, 10:279-285 II. The Children's Hospital, 11:310-315 III. Break, Break, Break, 12:320 IV. In the Valley of Cauteretz, 12:321 V. Wages, 12:321-322 VI. Crossing the Bar, 12:324 VII. Flower in the Crannied Wall, 13:280

2nd. I. Browning's Love Among the Ruins, 11:28-31 II. My Star, 12:58-59 III. From Pippa Passes, 12:59 IV. The Boy and the Angel, 11:133-137 V. Epilogue,

15: 143-144

3rd. H. C. BUNNER, b. 3 Ag. 1855 I. Behold the Deeds! 7-Pt. II:123-125 II. The Love Letters of Smith, 8-Pt. I:89-104

4th. PERCY BYSSHE SHELLEY, b. 4 Ag. 1792 I. The Sensitive Plant, 11:54-68 II. To Night, 12:43-44 III. The Indian Serenade, 12:159-160

5th. GUY DE MAUPASSANT, b. 5 Ag. 1850 I. The Piece of String, 21-Pt. II:96-106 II. The Necklace, 21-Pt. I:94-106

Plato is never sullen. Cervantes is never petulant. Demosthenes never comes unseasonably. Dante never stays too long. --LORD MACAULAY.

AUGUST 6th to 12th

6th. ALFRED TENNYSON, b. 6 Ag. 1809 I. Alfred Tennyson, 17-Pt. I:38-42 II. Dora, 11:11-17 III. The Lady of Shalott, 10:73-79

7th. JOSEPH RODMAN DRAKE, b. 7 Ag. 1795 I. Halleck's Joseph Rodman Drake, 15:104-105 II. Browning's Prospice, 15:145-146 III. Pied Piper, 11:163-173 IV. Meeting at Night, 12:189-190 V. Parting at Morning, 12:190

8th. SARA TEASDALE, b. 8 Ag. 1884 I. Teasdale's Blue Squills, 12:327 II. The Return, 12:338 III. Browning's Misconceptions, 12:190-191 IV. Rabbi Ben Ezra, 14:191-199

9th. JOHN DRYDEN, b. 9 Ag. 1631 I. Alexander's Feast, 13:63-70 II. Ah, How Sweet It Is to Love! 12:140-141 III. The Elixir, 15:150-151 IV. Discipline, 15:151-152 V. The Pulley, 15:153-154

10th. WITTER BYNNER, b. 10 Ag. 1881 I. Sentence, 13:295 II. Browning's Soul, 14:199-221 III. Herrick's To Blossoms, 12:33-34 IV. To Daffodils, 12:34 V. To Violets, 12:35

11th. I. Herrick's To Meadows, 12:35-36 II. Lacrim? 15:41-42 III. The Primrose, 12:124 IV. Litany, 15:158-160 V. Lowell's Madonna of the Evening Flowers, 11:319

12th. JAMES RUSSELL LOWELL, d. 12 Ag. 1891 I. Rhoecus, 11:127-13 3 II. The Courtin', 11:230-233 III. The Yankee Recruit, 7-Pt. I:52-60

Give us a house furnished with books rather than with furniture. Both if you can, but books at any rate! --HENRY WARD BEECHER.

AUGUST 13TH TO 19TH

13th. Battle of Blenheim, 13 Ag. 1704 I. Southey's After Blenheim, 10:192-194 II. De Quincey's Going Down with Victory, 4-Pt. II: 107-119

14th. JOHN FLETCHER, d. 14 Ag. 1785 I. Love's Emblems, 12:29-30 II. Hear, Ye Ladies, 12:132-133 III. Melancholy, 12:278-279 IV. Lodge's Rosalind's Madrigal, 12:83-84 V. Rosalind's Description, 12:84-86

15th. THOMAS DE QUINCEY, b. 15 Ag. 1785 I. The Pains of Opium, 4-Pt. II:73-100

16th. BARONESS NAIRNE (Carolina Oliphant), b. 16 Ag. 1766 I. The Laird o' Cockpen, 11:251-252 II. The Land o' the Leal, 12:311-312 III. Cather's Grandmither, Think Not I Forget, 14:313

17th. I. Ali Baba and the Forty Robbers, 19-Pt. II:1-58

18th. I. Longfellow's Rain in Summer, 14:96-99 II. Herrick's Corinna's Going a-Maying, 12:30-33 III. Shelley's Ode to the West Wind, 13:129-132

19th. Battle of Otterburn, 19 Ag. 1388 I. The Battle of Otterburn, 10:171-176

Books make up no small part of human happiness. --FREDERICK THE GREAT (in youth).

My latest passion will be for literature. --FREDERICK THE GREAT (in old age).

AUGUST 20TH TO 26TH

20th. MARCO BOZZARIS,fell 20 Ag. 1823 I. Halleck's Marco Bozzaris, 11:187-191 II. Lowell's Vision of Sir Launfal, 11:107-121

21st. MARY MAPES DODGE, d. 21 Ag. 1905 I. Miss Maloney on the Chinese Question, 7-Pt. 11:20-24 II. Lowell's Letter from a Candidate, 7-Pt. II:29-32

22nd. Royal Standard Raised at Nottingham, 22 Ag. 1642 I. Browning's Cavalier Tunes, 12:205-208 II. Milton's Il Penseroso, 14:14-19 III. Lycidas, 15:52-58

23rd. EDGAR LEE MASTERS, b. 23 Ag. 1869 I. Isaiah Beethoven, 14:308 II. Hardy's She Hears the Storm, 14:312 III. Wheelock's The Unknown Beloved, 10:309

24th. ROBERT HERRICK, baptized 24 Ag. 1591 I. To Dianeme, 12:123 II. Upon Julia's Clothes, 12:124 III. To the Virgins, to Make Much of Time, 12:125 IV. Delight in Disorder, 12:125-126 V. To Anthea, 12:126-127 VI. To Daisies, 12:127 VII. The Night Piece, 12:128

25th. BRET HARTE, b. 25 Ag. 1839 I. Plain Language from Truthful James, II:234-236 II. The Outcasts of Poker Flat, 20-Pt. I:30-46 III. Ramon, 11:285-288 IV. Her Letter, 8-Pt. I:113-115

26th. I. Holley's An Unmarried Female, 8-Pt. II: 26-36

We are as liable to be corrupted by books as by companions. --HENRY FIELDING.

27th. I. Scott's Coronach, 15:33-34 II. Lochinvar, 10:36-39 III. A Weary Lot Is Thine, 10:40-41 IV. County Guy, 12:154-155 V. Hail to the Chief, 12:203-204

28th. LEO TOLSTOI, b. 28 Ag. 1828 I. The Prisoner in the Caucasus, 19-Pt. I:141-186

29th. OLIVER WENDELL HOLMES,b. 29Ag. 1809;d. I. The Ballad of the Oysterman, 7-Pt. I:105-106 II. My Aunt, 7-Pt. I:23-24 III. Foreign Correspondence, 7-Pt. I:77-80 IV. The Chambered Nautilus, 14:108-109 The Royal George lost 29 Ag. 1782 V. Cowper's On the Loss of the Royal George, 10:148-149

30th. I. Scott's Brignall Banks, 10:41-43 II. Hunting Song, 12:230-231 III. Soldier Rest, 12:277-278 IV. Proud Maisie, 10:258 V. Harp of the North, 12:286-287

31st. TH 菋 PHILE GAUTIER, b. 31 Ag. 1811 I. The Mummy's Foot, 19-Pt. I:90-108

S. 1ST. SIMEON FORD, b. 31 Ag. 1855 I. At a Turkish Bath, 9-Pt. II:74-77 II. The Discomforts of Travel, 9-Pt. II: 123-127 III. Boyhood in a New England Hotel, 9-Pt. I:123-126

2nd. AUSTIN DOBSON, d. 2 S. 1921 I. Ballad of Prose and Rhyme, 12:335 II. Carman's Vagabond Song, 12:330 III. Colum's Old Woman of the Roads, 14:311 IV. Peabody's House and the Road, 12:344 V. Daly's Inscription for a Fireplace, 13:294

Old wood best to burn; old wine to drink; old friends to trust; and old authors to read. --ALONZO OF ARAGON.

SEPTEMBER 3RD TO 9TH

3rd. IVAN SERGEYEVICH TURGENIEFF, d. 3 S.1883 I. The Song of Triumphant Love, 19-Pt. I: 109-140 II. Wordsworth's Sonnet Composed Upon Westminster Bridge, Sept, 3, 1802, 13:211

4th. SIR RICHARD GRENVILLE, d. 4 (?) S. 1591 I. Tennyson's The Revenge, 10:222-229 II. Wordsworth's To the Skylark, 12:40-41 III. On a Picture of Peele Castle, 14:44-47

5th. I. Some Messages Received by Teachers in Brooklyn Public Schools, 7-Pt. II:144-147 II. Emerson's Labor, 2-Pt. I:138-145

6th. I. Wordsworth's Resolution and Independence, 11:48-54 II. Yarrow Unvisited, 14:53-55 III. Intimations of Immortality, 13:89-96 IV. Ode to Duty, 13:96-98 V. The Small Celandine, 14:112-113

7th. I. Milton's Echo, 12:25-26 II. Sabrina, 12:26-27 III. The Spirit's Epilogue, 12:27-29 IV. On Time, 13:52-53 V. At a Solemn Music, 13:53-54

8th. I. Wordsworth's Lucy, 15:114-118 II. Hart-Leap Well, 10:134-142 SIEGFRIED SASSOON, b. 8 S. 1886 III. Dreamers, 15:223

9th. SIR HUMPHREY GILBERT, drowned 9 S. 1583 I. Longfellow's Sir Humphrey Gilbert, 10:160-161 Battle of Flodden Field, 9 S. 1513 II. Elliot's A Lament for Flodden, 10:251-252 III. Wordsworth's Stepping Westward, 14:158-159 IV. She Was A Phantom of Delight, 14:159-160 V. Scorn Not the Sonnet, 13:175-176

To desire to have many books, and never use them, is like a child that will have a candle burning by him all the while he is sleeping. --HENRY PEACHAM.

SEPTEMBER 10TH TO 16TH

10th. I. Wordsworth's Nuns Fret Not, 13:175 II. Lines, 14:253-255 III. We Are Seven, 10:252-255

11th. JAMES THOMSON, b. II S. 1700 I. Rule Britannia, 12:208-209 II. Collins's On the Death of Thomson, 15:59-60 III. Lowell's A Winter Ride, 12:331 IV. MacKaye's The Automobile, 13:290

12th. CHARLES DUDLEY WARNER, b. 12 S. 1829 I. Plumbers, 8-Pt. I:150-151 II. My Summer in a Garden, 7-Pt. I:6l-74 III. How I Killed a Bear, 9-Pt. I:59-70

13th. GENERAL AMBROSE EVERETT BURNSIDE, d. 13 S. 1881 I. Lincoln's Letter to Burnside, 5-Pt. I:118 II. Collins's Ode Written in 1745, 15:34 III. The Passions, 13:81-85 IV. Ode to Evening, 13:85-88 V. Dirge in Cymbeline, 15:112-113

14th. DUKE OF WELLINGTON, d. 14 S. 1852 I. Tennyson's Ode on the Death of the Duke of Wellington, 13:151-161 DANTE, d. 14 S. 1321 II. Longfellow's Dante and Divina Comedia, 13:239-244 III. Parsons's On a Bust of Dante, 14:152-154

15th. I. Wordsworth's The Solitary Reaper, 14:160-161 II. Jonson's Hymn to Diana, 12:14 III. Pindaric Ode, 13:37-42 IV. Epitaph, 15:46-47 V. On Elizabeth L. H., 15:47

16th. ALFRED NOYES, b. 16 S. 1880 I. Old Grey Squirrel, 14:306 JOHN GAY, baptized 16 S. 1685 II. Black-Eyed Susan, 10:32-34 CHARLES BATTELL LOOMIS, b. 16 S. 1861 III. O-U-G-H, 7-Pt. I:143

It does not matter how many, but how good, books you have. --SENECA.

SEPTEMBER 17TH to 23RD

17th. I. Turner's The Harvest Moon, 13:249 II. Letty's Globe, 13:245-246 III. Mary, A Reminiscence, 13:246-247 IV. Her First-born, 13:247-248 V. The

Lattice at Sunrise, 13:248

18th. DR. SAMUEL JOHNSON, b. 18 S. 1709 I. Macaulay's Dr. Samuel Johnson, 2-Pt. II:39-79

19th. HARTLEY COLERIDGE, b. 19 S. 1796 I. Song, 12:166-167 II. Sonnets, 13:227-230 III. Coleridge's Frost at Midnight, 14:22-25 IV. Love, 10:44-47 V. France: An Ode, 13:99-103

20th. WILLIAM HAINES LYTLE, d. 20 S. 1863 I. Antony to Cleopatra, 14:238-240 II. Hood's The Death Bed, 15:131 III. Autumn, 13:148-150 IV. Ruth, 14:157-158 V. Fair Ines, 12:168-169

21st. SIR WALTER SCOTT, d. 21 S. 1832 I. Sir Walter Scott, 17-Pt. I:65-73 II. The Maid of Neidpath, 10:39-40 III. Pibroch of Donald Dhu, 12:201-203 IV. Wandering Willie's Tale, 20-Pt. II:75-103

22nd. I. Wordsworth's My Heart Leaps Up, 13:274 II. Laodamia, 11:143-150 III. There Was a Boy, 14:156-157

23rd. Battle of Monterey, 23 S. 1846 I. Hoffman's Monterey, 10:206-207 II. Lovelace's The Grasshopper, 12:30 III. To Lucasta, 12:129-130 IV. To Althea, 12:130-131 V. To Lucasta, on Going to the Wars, 12:198

The words of the good are like a staff in a slippery place. --HINDU SAYING.

SEPTEMBER 24TH TO 30TH

24th. I. Noyes's Creation, 15:204

25th. FELICIA DOROTHEA HEMANS, b. 25 S. 1793 I. Landing of the Pilgrim Fathers, 10:151-153 II. Poe's Annabel Lee, 10:56-57 III. To Helen, 12:176 IV. The Bells, 12:234-238 V. For Annie, 12:305-308

26th. I. Holmes's Latter-Day Warnings, 7-Pt. I:34-35 II. Contentment, 7-Pt. I:35-38 III. An Aphorism, 8-Pt. II:44-52 IV. Music Pounding, 7-Pt. I:80-81

27th. I. Holmes's The Height of the Ridiculous, 8-Pt. I:118-119 II. The Last Leaf, 14:167-168 III. The One-Hoss Shay, 11:236-241

28th. I. Morley's Haunting Beauty of Strychnine, 9-Pt. I:135 II. Guiterman's Strictly Germ-Proof, 7-Pt. I:141 III. Burgess's Lazy Roof, 8-Pt. I:149 IV. My Feet, 8-Pt. I:149

29th. EMILE ZOLA, d. 29 S. 1902 I. The Death of Olivier, 21-Pt. I:53-93

30th. I. Lowell's Without and Within, 8-Pt. II:72-73 II. She Came and Went, 15:134 III. The Sower, 14:144-145 IV. Sonnets, 13:251-253 V. What Rabbi Jehosha Said, 14:282-283

If you are reading a piece of thoroughly good literature, Baron Rothschild may possibly be as well occupied as you--he is certainly not better occupied. --P. G. HAMERTON.

OCTOBER 1ST TO 7TH

1st. LOUIS UNTERMYER, b. 1 O. 1885 I. Only of Thee and Me, 12:339 II. Morris's October, 14:105-106 III. Bunner's Candor, 8-Pt. I:11-12

2nd. French Fleet destroyed off Boston, October, 1746 I. Longfellow's Ballad of the French Fleet, 10:202-204 II. Mrs. Browning's Sleep, 15:21-23 III. The Romance of the Swan's Nest, 10:79-83 IV. A Dead Rose, 12:191-192 V. A Man's Requirements, 12:192-194

3rd. WILLIAM MORRIS, d. 3 O. 1896 I. Summer Dawn, 12:172 II. The Nymph's Song to Hylas, 12:173-174 III. The Voice of Toil, 12:290-292 IV. The Shameful Death, 10:277-279

4th. HENRY CAREY, d. 4 O. 1743 I. Sally in Our Alley, 12:142-144 II. Van Dyke's The Proud Lady, 10:296

5th. I. Poe's Ulalume, II:302-306 II. Arnold's The Last Word, 15:43 III. A Nameless Epitaph, 15:48 IV. Thyrsis, 15:86-97 V. Requiescat, 15:120-121

6th. GEORGE HENRY BOKER, b. 6 O. 1893 I. The Black Regiment, 10:207-210 II. Lamb's Letter to Wordsworth, 5-Pt. II:129-132 III. Letter to Wordsworth, 5-Pt. II:136-143 IV. Letter to Wordsworth, 5-Pt. II:143-145

7th. SIR PHILIP SIDNEY, d. 7 O. 1586 I. The Bargain, 12:87 II. Astrophel and Stella, 13:178-180 III. To Sir Philip Sidney's Soul, 13:181 EDGAR ALLAN POE, d. 7 O. 1849 IV. The Murders in the Rue Morgue, Pt. I:1-53

A little before you go to sleep read something that is exquisite and worth remembering; and contemplate upon it till you fall asleep. --ERASMUS.

OCTOBER 8TH TO 14TH

8th. JOHN HAY, b. 8 O. 1838 I. Little Breeches, 7-Pt. I:45-47 EDMUND CLARENCE STEDMAN, b. 8 O. 1833. II. The Diamond Wedding, 7-Pt. I:107-114

9th. S. W. GILLILAN, b. O. 1869 I. Finnigin to Flannigan, 9-Pt. I:92-93 II. Dunne's On Expert Testimony, 9-Pt. II:13-16 III. Work and Sport, 9-Pt. II:87-92 IV. Avarice and Generosity, 9-Pt. II:144-146

10th. WILLIAM H. SEWARD, d. 10 0. 1872 I. Lincoln's Letter to Seward, 5-Pt. I:111-112 II. Walker's Medicine Show, 18:213

11th. I. Keats's To Autumn, 13:142-143 II. Carew's Epitaph, 15:48 III. Disdain Returned, 12:133-134 IV. Song, 12:134 V. To His Inconstant Mistress, 12:135

12th. ROBERT E. LEE, d. 12 O. 1870 I. Robert E. Lee, 16-Pt. II:62-73 DINAH MULOCK CRAIK, d. 12 O. 1887. II. Douglas, Douglas, Tender and True 12:310-

311

13th. SIR HENRY IRVING, d. 13 O. 1905 I. Sir Henry Irving, 17-Pt. II:39-47

14th. JOSH BILLINGS (H. W. SHAW), d. 14 O. 1885 I. Natral and Unnatral Aristokrats, 7-Pt. I:48-51 II. To Correspondents, 9-Pt. I:73-74 III. Russell's Origin of the Banjo, 9-Pt. I:79-82

And when a man is at home and happy with a book, sitting by his fireside, he must be a churl if he does not communicate that happiness. Let him read now and then to his wife and children. --H. FRISWELL.

OCTOBER 15TH TO 21ST

15th. I. Tennyson's Tears, Idle Tears, 12:272-273 II. Shakespeare's Over Hill, Over Dale, 12:19 III. Poe's Assignation, 4-Pt. I:81-101

16th. I. Nye's How to Hunt the Fox, 8-Pt. I:70-78 II. A Fatal Thirst, 7-Pt. II:148-150 III. On Cyclones, 9-Pt. I:83-85

17th. WILLIAM VAUGHN MOODY, d. 17 O. 1910 I. Gloucester Moors, 11:320

18th. THOMAS LOVE PEACOCK, b. 18 O. 1785 I. Three Men of Gotham, 12:257-258 II. Shakespeare's Silvia, 12:91-92 III. O Mistress Mine, 12:92 IV. Take, O Take Those Lips Away, 12:93 V. Love, 12:93-94

19th. LEIGH HUNT, b. 19 O. 1784 I. Jenny Kissed Me, 12:158 II. Abou Ben Adhem, 11:121-122 CORNWALLIS surrendered at Yorktown, 19 O. 1781 III. Tennyson's England and America in 1782, 12:209-210

20th. I. Shakespeare's The Fairy Life, 12:20 II. When Icicles Hang by the Wall, 12:22 III. Fear No More the Heat of the Sun, 15:37 IV. A Sea Dirge, 15:38

21st. SAMUEL TAYLOR COLERIDGE, b. 21 0. 1772 I. Youth and Age, 14:264-

265 II. Kubla Khan, 14:80-82 III. Thompson's Arab Love Song, 12:339

I wist all their sport in the Park is but a shadow to that pleasure I find in Plato. Alas! good folk, they never felt what true pleasure meant. --ROGER ASCHAM.

OCTOBER 22ND TO 28TH

22nd. I. Shakespeare's Crabbed Age and Youth, 12:94 II. On A Day, Alack the Day, 12:95 III. Come Away, Come Away, Death, 12:96 IV. Rittenhouse's Ghostly Galley, 13:296 V. O'Hara's Atropos, 15:199

23rd. I. Townsend's Chimmie Fadden Makes Friends, 9-Pt. I:105-109 II. Tompkins's Sham, 18:169

24th. I. Tarkington's Beauty and the Jacobin, 18:19

25th. THOMAS BABINGTON MACAULAY, b 25 O. 1800 I. Country Gentlemen, 2-Pt. II:110-119 II. Polite Literature, 2-Pt. II:119-132 Battle of Balaclava, 25 O. 1854. III. Tennyson's Charge of the Light Brigade, 10:217-219 IV. Tennyson's Charge of the Heavy Brigade, 10:219-221

26th. I. Vaughan's Friends Departed, 15:10-11 II. Peace, 15:160-161 III. The Retreat, 15:161-162 IV. The World, 14:245-247

27th. THEODORE ROOSEVELT, b. 27 0. 1858 I. Colonel Theodore Roosevelt, 16-Pt. II:74-94

28th. I. Zola's Attack on the Mill, 20-Pt. I:47-102

I never think of the name of Gutenberg without feelings of veneration and homage. --G. S. PHILLIPS.

OCTOBER 29TH TO NOVEMBER 4TH

29th. JOHN KEATS, b. 29 O. 1795 I. Ode on a Grecian Urn, 13:137-139 II. The Eve of St. Agnes, 11:68-83

30th. ADELAIDE ANNE PROCTER, b. 30 O. 1825 I. A Doubting Heart, 12:312-313 II. Marlowe's Passionate Shepherd, 12:97-98 III. Raleigh's Her Reply, 12:98-99 IV. The Pilgrimage, 12:314-316

31st. Hallowe'en I. Burns's Tam O'Shanter, 11:253-260

N. 1st. I. Bryant's The Death of the Flowers, 14:118-120 II. The Battle-Field, 15:26-28 III. The Evening Wind, 12:50-52 IV. To a Waterfowl, 13:147-148

2nd. I. Arnold's Rugby Chapel, 15: 97-104 II. Campion's Cherry-Ripe, 12:103 III. Follow Your Saint, 12:103-104 IV. Vobiscum est Iope, 12:105

3rd. WILLIAM CULLEN BRYANT, b. 3 N. 1794 I. The Mosquito, 8-Pt. II:58-61 II. To the Fringed Gentian, 14:114-115 III. Song of Marion's Men, 10:199-201 IV. Forest Hymn, 14:34-38

4th. EUGENE FIELD, d. 4 N. 1895 I. Baked Beans and Culture, 9-Pt. I:86-89 II. The Little Peach, 8-Pt. I:86 III. Dibdin's Ghost, 9-Pt. II:44-46 IV. Dutch Lullaby, 12:250-251

To divert myself from a troublesome Fancy 'tis but to run to my books ... they always receive me with the same kindness. --MONTAIGNE.

NOVEMBER 5TH TO 11TH

5th. I. Lowell's What Mr. Robinson Thinks, 7-Pt. I:115-117 II. Field's The Truth About Horace, 9-Pt. I:17-18 III. The Cyclopeedy, 9-Pt. I:127-134

6th. HOLMAN F. DAY, b. 6 N. 1865 I. Tale of the Kennebec Mariner, 9-Pt. II:10-12 II. Grampy Sings a Song, 9-Pt. II:64-66 III. Cure for Homesickness, 9-Pt.

II:129-130 IV. The Night After Christmas (Anonymous), 9-Pt. I:75-76

7th. I. Gibson's The Fear, 15:216 II. Back, 15:216 III. The Return, 15:217

8th. JOHN MILTON, d. 8 N. 1674 I. Sonnets, 13:198-205 II. L'Allegro, 14:9-14 III. On Milton by Dryden, 13:272

9th. I. Lincoln's Letter to Astor, Roosevelt, and Sands, 9 N. 1863, 5-Pt. I:119 II. Arnold's Saint Brandan, II:137-140 III. Longing, 12:188-189 IV. Sonnets, 13:253-256

10th. HENRY VAN DYKE, b. 10 N. 1852 I. Salute to the Trees, 14:290 II. The Standard Bearer, 10:307 VACHEL LINDSAY, b. 10 N. 1879 III. Abraham Lincoln Walks at Midnight, 14:298

11th. Armistice Day, 11 N. 1918 I. Wharton's The Young Dead, 15:213 II. Meynell's Dead Harvest, 14:292 III. Tennyson's Locksley Hall, 14:223-238

We have known Book-love to be independent of the author and lurk in a few charmed words traced upon the title-page by a once familiar hand. -- ANONYMOUS.

NOVEMBER 12TH TO 18TH

12th. RICHARD BAXTER, b. 12 N. 1615 I. A Hymn of Trust, 15:164-165 II. Arnold's The Future, 14:275-278 III. Palladium, 14:278-279 IV. The Forsaken Merman, 11:291-296

13th. ROBERT LOUIS STEVENSON, b. 13 N. 1850 I. Robert Louis Stevenson, 17-Pt. I:133-146 II. Foreign Lands, 12:248-249 III. Requiem, 15:142

14th. BOOKER T. WASHINGTON, d. 14 N. 1915 I. Booker T. Washington, 17-Pt. I:172-190

15th. WILLIAM COWPER, b. 26 N. 1731 I. To Mary, 12:243-245 II. Boadicea, 10:181-182 III. Verses, 14:221-223 IV. Diverting History of John Gilpin, 11:241-251

16th. I. Cone's Ride to the Lady, 10:311 II. Hewlett's Soldier, Soldier, 15:212

17th. Lucknow relieved by Campbell, 17 N. 1857 I. Robert Lowell's The Relief of Lucknow, 11:184-187 II. Roberts's The Maid, 10:305

18th. I. Joseph Conrad, 17-Pt. I:147-166

Read not to contradict and confute, nor to believe and take for granted, nor to find talk and discourse, but to weigh and consider. --LORD BACON.

NOVEMBER 19TH TO 25TH

19th. I. Lincoln's Gettyburg Address, 5-Pt. I: 107-108

20th. THOMAS CHATTERTON, b. 20 N. 1752 I. Minstrel's Song, 15:40-41 CHARLES GRAHAM HALPINE, b. 20 N. 1829 II. Irish Astronomy, 8-Pt. II:79-80 III. Davis's The First Piano in a Mining-Camp, 9-Pt. I:34-44 IV. Dunne's On Gold Seeking, 9-Pt. I:99-102

21st. VOLTAIRE, b. 21 N. 1694 I. Jeannot and Colin, 22-Pt. I:1-16 BRYAN WALLER PROCTER (Barry Cornwall), b. 21 N. 1787 II. The Sea, 12:72-73 III. The Poet's Song to His Wife, 12:242-243 IV. A Petition to Time, 12:252

22nd. St. Cecilia's Day, Nov. 22nd. I. Dryden's Song for St. Cecilia's Day, 13:61-63 II. O May I Join the Choir Invisible, 15:185-186 JACK LONDON, d. 22 N. 1916 III. Jan the Unrepentant, 22-Pt. II:136

23rd. I. Carryl's The Walloping Window Blind, 9-Pt. II:35-36 II. Marble's The Hoosier and the Salt-pile, 8-Pt. II:62-67

24th. I. Arnold's Growing Old, 14:281-282 II. Lyly's Spring's Welcome, 12:15 III. Cupid and Campaspe, 12:86 IV. Lindsay's Auld Robin Gray, 10:30-32

25th. I. Irving's The Devil and Tom Walker, 3-Pt. II:37-57

Montaigne with his sheepskin blistered, And Howell the worse for wear, And the worm-drilled Jesuit's Horace, And the little old cropped Moliere-- And the Burton I bought for a florin, And the Rabelais foxed and flea'd-- For the others I never have opened, But those are the ones I read. --AUSTIN DOBSON.

NOVEMBER 26th TO DECEMBER 2ND

26th. COVENTRY PATMORE, d. 26 N. 1896 I. To the Unknown Eros, 13:169-171 II. The Toys, 15:140-141 III. Lamb's The Old Familiar Faces, 15:73-74 IV. Hester, 15:75-76

27th. I. Wordsworth's Influence of Natural Objects, 14:251-253 RIDGELEY TORRENCE, b. 27 N. 1875 II. Torrence's Evensong, 12:346 III. Burt's Resurgam, 13:292

28th. WILLIAM BLAKE, b. 28 N. 1757 I. The Tiger, 12:42-43 II. Piping Down the Valleys, 12:246 III. The Golden Door, 15:172 WASHINGTON IRVING. d. 28 N. 1859 IV. Rip Van Winkle, 19-Pt. II:71-96

29th. LOUISA MAY ALCOTT, b. 29 N. 1832 I. Street Scenes in Washington, 8-Pt. II:74-76 JOHN G. NEIHARDT, married 29 N. 1908 II. Envoi, 15:200 III. Cheney's Happiest Heart, 14:318 IV. Dargan's There's Rosemary, 13:287

30th. SAMUEL LANGHORNE CLEMENS (Mark Twain), b. 30 N. 1835 I. Colonel Mulberry Sellers, 7-Pt. II:31-40 II. The Notorious Jumping Frog, 7-Pt. I:122-131

D. 1st. I. Keats's In a Drear-Nighted December, 12:268 II. Gray's Progress of Poesy, 13:76-80 III. Doyle's Private of the Buffs, 11:284-285

2nd. I. Lowell's The First Snow-Fail, 15:135-136 II. Daniel's Love Is a Sickness, 12:108 III. Delia, 13:181-182 IV. Darley's Song, 12:170-171

When evening has arrived, I return home, and go into my study.... For hours together, the miseries of life no longer annoy me; I forget every vexation; I do not fear poverty; for I have altogether transferred myself to those with whom I hold converse. --MACHIAVELLI.

DECEMBER 3RD TO 9TH

3rd. GEORGE B. MCCLELLAN, b. 3 D. 1826 I. Lincoln's Letter to McClellan, 5-Pt. I:109-110 Battle of Hohenlinden, 3 D. 1800 II. Campbell's Hohenlinden, 10:188-189 ROBERT Louis STEVENSON, d. 3 D. 1894 III. Providence and the Guitar, 19-Pt. II: 96-138

4th. I. Sudermann's The Gooseherd, 20-Pt. II:62-74

5th. CHRISTINA GEORGINA ROSSETTI, b. 5 D. 1830 I. One Certainty, 13:265 II. Up-Hill, 12:322-323 III. Hayne's In Harbor, 15:142-143 IV. Between the Sunken Sun and the New Moon, 13:265-266 V. Goldsmith's When Lovely Woman Stoops to Folly, 13:273

6th. R. H. BARHAM, b. 6 D. 1788 I. The Jackdaw of Rheims, 11:173-179

7th. CALE YOUNG RICE, b. 7 D. 1872 I. Chant of the Colorado, 14:291 ALLAN CUNNINGHAM, b. 7 D. 1784 II. A Wet Sheet and a Flowing Sea, 12:73-74 III. Hame, Hame, Hame, 12:309-310 IV. Bailey's After the Funeral, 8-Pt. I:42-44 V. What He Wanted It For, 9-Pt. I:90-91

8th. I. A Visit to Brigham Young, 9-Pt. I:47-52

9th. STEPHEN PHILLIPS, d. 9 D. 1915 I. Harold before Senlac, 14:315

This habit of reading, I make bold to tell you, is your pass to the greatest, the purest, and the most perfect pleasures that God has prepared for his creatures.... It lasts when all other pleasures fade. --TROLLOPE.

DECEMBER 10TH TO 16TH

10th. EMILY DICKINSON, b. 10 D. 1830 I. Our Share of Night to Bear, 13:282 II. Heart, We Will Forget Him, 13:282 III. Ruskin's Mountain Glory, 1-Pt. II:59-69

11th. I. Webster's Reply to Hayne, 6-Pt. I:63-105

12th. I. Herford's Gold, 9-Pt. II:9 II. Child's Natural History, 9-Pt. II:37-39 III. Metaphysics, 9-Pt. II:128 IV. The End of the World, 9-Pt. I:120-122

13th. WILLIAM DRUMMOND, b. 13 D. 1585 I. Invocation, 12:24-25 II. "I Know That All Beneath the Moon Decays," 13:196-197 III. For the Baptist, 13:197 IV. To His Lute, 13:198 V. Browne's The Siren's Song, 12:23 VI. A Welcome, 12:111-112 VII. My Choice, 12:112-113

14th. CHARLES WOLFE, b. 14 D. 1791 I. The Burial of Sir John Moore, 15:31-33 II. Clough's In a Lecture Room, 14:272 III. Qua Cursum Ventus, 12:317-318 IV. Davis's Souls, 14:317

15th. I. Mrs. Browning's Sonnets from the Portuguese, 13:232-239

16th. GEORGE SANTAYANA, b. 16 D. 1863 I. "As in the Midst of Battle There Is Room," 13:287 II. MacMillan's Shadowed Star, 18:273

When there is no recreation or business for thee abroad, thou may'st have a company of honest old fellows in their leathern jackets in thy study which will find thee excellent divertisement at home. --THOMAS FULLER.

DECEMBER 17TH TO 23RD

17th. JOHN GREENLEAF WHITTIER, b. 17 D. 1807 I. Amy Wentworth, 10:53-56 II. The Barefoot Boy, 14:169-172 III. My Psalm, 15:180-191 IV. The Eternal Goodness, 15:192-196 V. Telling the Bees, 11:308-310

18th. PHILIP FRENEAU, d. 18 D. 1832 I. The Wild Honeysuckle, 14:113-114 L. G. C. A. CHATRIAN, b. 18 D. 1826 II. The Comet, 20-Pt. II:104-114

19th. BAYARD TAYLOR, d. 19 D. 1878 I. Palabras Grandiosas, 9-Pt. I:58 II. Bedouin Love Song, 12:174-175 III. The Song of the Camp, 11:288-290 IV. W. B. Scott's Glenkindie, 10:48-51

20th. I. Ford's The Society Reporter's Christmas, 8-Pt. I:57-65 II. The Dying Gag, 9-Pt. II:119-122

21st. GIOVANNI BOCCACCIO, d. 21 D. 1375 I. The Falcon, 20-Pt. II:1-11

22nd. EDWIN ARLINGTON ROBINSON, b. 22 D. 1869 I. Miniver Cheevy, 7-Pt. I:147 II. Vickery's Mountain, 14:303 III. Richard Cory, 14:309

23rd. MICHAEL DRAYTON, d. 23 D. 1631 I. Idea, 13:182 II. Agincourt, 10:176-181 III. Stevenson's The Whaups, 12:70 IV. Youth and Love, 12:231

Life being very short, and the quiet hours of it few, we ought to waste none of them in reading valueless books; and valuable books should, in a civilized country, be within the reach of every one. --JOHN RUSKIN.

DECEMBER 24TH TO 31ST

24th. Christmas Eve I. Guiney's Tryste No, 15:202 II. Rossetti's My Sister's Sleep, 15:137-139 MATTHEW ARNOLD, b. 24 D. 1822 III. Dover Beach, 14:279-280 IV. Philomela, 12:56-57

25th. I. Milton's Ode on The Morning of Christ's Nativity, 13:42-43 II. Thackeray's The Mahogany Tree, 12:252-254 III. Thackeray's The End of the

Play, 14:283-286 IV. Domett's A Christmas Hymn, 15:178-179

26th. THOMAS GRAY, b. 26 D. 1716 I. Elegy, 15:12-17 II. Ode to Adversity, 13:70-72 III. Ode on a Distant Prospect of Eton College, 13:72-76

27th. CHARLES LAMB, d. 27 D. 1834 I. Landor's To the Sister of Elia, 15:76-77 II. A Dissertation upon Roast Pig, 5-Pt. II:40-51 III. Detached Thoughts on Books and Reading, 5-Pt. II 70-79

28th. I. Hawthorne's The Birthmark, 3-Pt. I:23-51

29th. JOHN VANCE CHENEY, b,. 29 D. 1848 I. Cheney's Happiest Heart, 14:318 II. Emerson's Terminus, 14:267-268 III. Clough's Say Not the Struggle Nought Availeth, 14:272-273 IV. Lamb's Old Familiar Faces, 15:73-74

30th. RUDYARD KIPLING, b. 30 D. 1865 I. Without Benefit of Clergy, 19-Pt. I:54-89

31st. I. Shelley's The World's Great Age Begins Anew, 12:284-286 II. Burns's Auld Lang Syne, 12:261-262 III. Lowell's To the Past, 13:161-163 IV. Lamb's New Year's Eve, 5-Pt. II:11-21

www.ingramcontent.com/pod-product-compliance
Lightning Source LLC
Chambersburg PA
CBHW062018280526
45787CB00005B/2156